FACTS AT YOUR FINGERTIPS

INTRODUCING PHYSICS
MECHANICS

BROWN BEAR BOOKS

CONTENTS

Published by Brown Bear Books Limited

4877 N. Circulo Bujia
Tucson, AZ 85718
USA
and
First Floor
9-17 St. Albans Place
London N1 ONX
UK
www.brownreference.com

© 2010 The Brown Reference Group Ltd

Library of Congress Cataloging-in-Publication Data

Mechanics / edited By Graham Bateman.
     p. cm. – (Facts at your fingertips)
   Includes index.
   ISBN 978-1-936333-09-7 (lib. bdg.)
 1. Mechanics–Juvenile literature. 2. Matter–Properties–Juvenile literature.
3. Physics–Juvenile literature. I. Bateman, Graham. II. Title: Mechanics. III.
Series.

QC127.4.I58 2010
531–dc22

                            2010015491

ISBN-13 978-1-936333-09-7

Editorial Director: Lindsey Lowe
Project Director: Graham Bateman
Design Manager: David Poole
Designer: Steve McCurdy
Picture Researchers: Steve McCurdy, Graham Bateman
Text Editors: Peter Lewis, Briony Ryles
Indexer: David Bennett
Children's Publisher: Anne O'Daly
Production Director: Alastair Gourlay

Printed in the United States of America

Picture Credits
Abbreviations: SS=Shutterstock; c=center; t=top; l=left; r=right.

Cover Images
Front: SS Back: SS

1 SS: Joker pro; 3 Great Images in NASA; 4 Photos.com; 6-7
Photos.com; 8 SS: Comptine; 10 Photos.com; 12-13 Great Images in
NASA; 18 Wikimedia Commons: United States Department of
Energy; 21 Great Images in NASA; 22 SS: Alfred Wekelo; 24-25 SS:
Drazen Vulelic; 26 Wikimedia Commons: U.S. Navy; 28 SS: Jonathan
Larsen; 32 SS: Jokerpro; 34 Photos.com; 37 SS: Belinda Pretorius; 38
SS: Photo Storm; 39 SS: Vorm in Beeld; 40-41 SS: Andrey Bannov; 42
Wikimedia Commons: Ahodges7; 45 Wikimedia Commons:
Nagyman; 47 SS: Suzanne Tucker; 47 SS: LianeM; 48 SS: Victor I.
Makhanokov; 50 SS: Zbynek; 51 SS: Devi; 52-53 Wikimedia
Commons: U.S. Navy; 55 SS: Semjonow Juri; 56-57 SS: Caarsten
Medorn Madsen; 58-59 SS: PBB.cz (Richard Semik).

Artwork © The Brown Reference Group Ltd

*The Brown Reference Group Ltd has made every effort to trace
copyright holders of the pictures used in this book. Anyone having
claims to ownership not identified above is invited to contact The
Brown Reference Group Ltd.*

Facts at your Fingertips—Introducing Physics describes the processes and practical implications fundamental to the study of physics. Much of physics concerns the movement of objects, and in order for something to move a force must be involved. When the forces are in equilibrium an object will be stationary. The branch of physics that deals with forces and movement is called mechanics, and is the primary subject of this volume. The volume also includes sections on measurement of matter, the fine detail of matter at the atomic level, energy, work, and power, as well as descriptions of levers and other simple machines, and the strain that can be exerted on fixed solids.

Numerous explanatory diagrams and informative photographs, detailed features on related aspects of the topics covered and the main scientists involved in the advancement of physics, and definitions of key "Science Words," all enhance the coverage. "Try This" features outline experiments that can be undertaken as a first step to practical investigations.

MEASURING MATTER

Measurement is at the heart of physics. Indeed, observation and measurement are central to the whole of science. Measurement requires units to express how heavy, how long, or how old something is. Science uses a wide range of units that measure everything from the size of an atom to the age of the universe.

In everyday life we use a variety of units, usually chosen to suit the thing that we are measuring. For instance, we measure the distance to the next town or city in miles, the size of a parking lot in yards, the height of a flagpole in feet, and the size of a piece of paper in inches. These are all units of length—distance is simply a length along the ground, and height is a length measured in an upward direction.

But such a mixture of units can be a nuisance, as we find out when we have to do the math involved in changing inches to feet or yards to miles. Also, the miles used in the United States may be different from the miles used in Finland or in China. U.S. pints and gallons are different from British pints and gallons.

These sausage-shaped objects are Salmonella *bacteria, each about a micrometer long. They are shown here magnified about 100,000 times in an artificially colored image taken by a scanning electron microscope (SEM).*

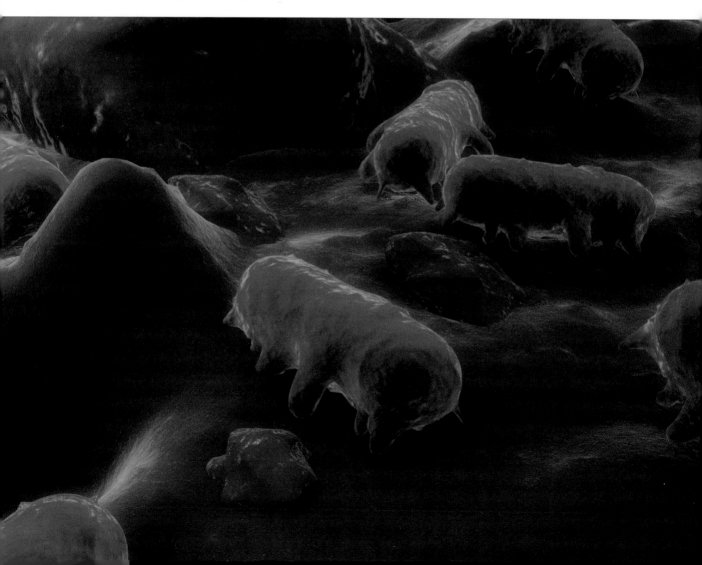

SI SYSTEM OF UNITS

Shown below are the seven base units of the SI system, which are supplemented by radians and steradians for measuring angles in advanced math (1 radian equals about 57 degrees). Among the important derived units are the hertz, used for measuring frequency; the newton, for measuring force; the ohm, volt, and watt used for measuring electrical resistance, voltage, and power, respectively; and the joule, for measuring energy.

	Mass	Amount of substance	Length	Current	Luminous intensity	Temperature	Time
SI unit	kilogram	mole	meter	ampere	candela	kelvin	second
Symbol	kg	mol	m	A	cd	K	s

SCIENCE WORDS

- **Luminous intensity:** The light-emitting power of a source of light.
- **Mass:** The amount of matter in an object.
- **SI units:** System of units used internationally in science (short for *Système International d'Unités*, its name in French). There are seven base units (ampere, candela, kelvin, kilogram, meter, mole, and second) and various derived units, which are combinations of base units.
- **Standard form:** A way of expressing very large or very small numbers that uses an index to represent powers of 10. For example, 10,000,000 is 10^7 and 0.000002 is $2 * 10^{-6}$.

For example, 1 U.S. pint equals 0.473 liters, while 1 British pint equals 0.568 liters (the British pint is bigger than the U.S. pint). The British gallon is also 1.2 times larger than the U.S. gallon. Scientists get around these problems by having only one unit for length—the meter. Every length is measured in meters or in multiples of meters (for example, kilometers) or in submultiples of meters (for example, centimeters).

To make the multiples and submultiples there are a number of standard prefixes that go before the word for the base unit. For example, the prefix *kilo-* means "1,000 times:" 1 kilometer = 1,000 meters (written as 1 km = 1,000 m). In a similar way, *centi-* means "1/100:" 1 centimeter (1 cm) = 1/100 meter (0.01 m). Thus the distance from Chicago to Los Angeles is about 1,740 km; the length of a new pencil is about 18 cm. There is a list of these prefixes on page 7.

The metric system

The meter is a unit in the metric system. This system was invented in France about 200 years ago, when the meter was taken to be a ten-millionth of the distance from the Equator to the North Pole along the Paris meridian. The kilogram is also a metric unit. The metric system is used for everyday measurements in most European countries and is becoming increasingly common in the United States.

Science uses a version of the metric system called the SI system (so called after its French name, *Système*

The illustration below shows some old types of measuring instruments:
(a) Human forearm, about 0.5 meter long. (b) Simple balance for
weighing. (c) Water clock for telling time. (d) Sundial for telling
time of day. (e) Astrolabe for measuring angles of stars. (f) Hourglass
for measuring elapsed time. (g) Micrometer for measuring small
thicknesses. (h) Sextant for measuring the Sun's angle in the sky.

METRIC PREFIXES

Prefix	Symbol	Multiple	Prefix	Symbol	Multiple	Prefix	Symbol	Multiple
atto-	a	$* 10^{-18}$	centi-	c	$* 10^{-2}$	mega-	M	$* 10^{6}$
femto-	f	$* 10^{-15}$	deci-	d	$* 10^{-1}$	giga-	G	$* 10^{9}$
pico-	p	$* 10^{-12}$	deca-	da	$* 10$	tera-	T	$* 10^{12}$
nano-	n	$* 10^{-9}$	hecto-	h	$* 10^{2}$	peta-	P	$* 10^{15}$
micro-	μ	$* 10^{-6}$	kilo-	k	$* 10^{3}$	exa-	E	$* 10^{18}$
milli-	m	$* 10^{-3}$						

Here are some examples:

picofarad (pF), equal to 10^{-12} farads, used to measure capacitance
nanometer (nm), equal to 10^{-9} meters, used to measure molecules
microampere (μA), equal to 10^{-6} amperes, used to measure nerve impulses
milligram (mg), equal to 10^{-3} grams, used to weigh out medicines
centiliter (cl), equal to 10^{-2} liters, used to measure wine
hectare (ha), equal to 10^{2} ares, used for areas of fields
kilovolt (kV), equal to 10^{3} volts, used for railroad voltages
megawatt (MW), equal to 10^{6} watts, used for a power-plant output
gigabyte (Gb), equal to 10^{9} bytes, used for computer storage capacity

A pole vaulter clears the bar at a track-and-field contest. Athletes' achievements are measured in metric units. The world women's high jump record is more than 5 meters (16.4 feet).

An atomic clock, such as this, keeps time to an accuracy of better than 1 second in 30,000 years.

International d'Unités). This system has seven base units, shown at the top of page 5, two supplementary, and various derived units. There are 18 derived units, each with a special name and made from combinations of the seven base units. The base unit of mass is the kilogram (= 1,000 grams), chosen because the gram (about 1/30 oz) is too small for many measurements. Throughout this book we usually give measurements both in SI and their customary equivalents, but sometimes only in SI units when this is most relevant.

Standard form

When measurements are made using SI or metric units, some of the numbers become very large indeed. For example, the Earth lies about 150 million km from the Sun, which in figures is 150,000,000 km. Standard form uses an index to express large numbers as powers of 10. For instance, $1,000 = 10^{3}$ and $1,000,000 = 10^{6}$. So the distance to the Sun is $1.5 * 10^{8}$ km. A human hair is about a ten-thousandth of a meter across, or 0.0001 m. In standard form this is written as $1 * 10^{-4}$ m.

MEASURING TEMPERATURE

Temperatures are measured using a thermometer, which is a device that utilizes some property of a substance that changes when the substance is heated. For instance, the common liquid-in-glass thermometer makes use of the fact that a liquid expands when heated. Another type makes use of the expansion of a metal when it is heated.

To express an object's level of hotness, we need a temperature scale and also a temperature-measuring device—a thermometer. The familiar mercury thermometer is a long, narrow glass tube with a bulb at one end that contains mercury. The other end of the tube is sealed. When the bulb is heated (by being placed where the temperature is to be measured), the mercury inside it expands and so moves along the tube. The distance it moves gives a measure of the temperature. The glass tube is graduated in degrees, either in Fahrenheit or Celsius.

SCIENCE WORDS

- **Bimetallic strip:** A strip consisting of two different metals bonded together. The metals expand at different rates when they are heated, so the strip bends when it is heated.
- **Celsius scale:** A temperature scale that has 100 degrees between the freezing point of water (0°C) and the boiling point of water (100°C). It used to be called the centigrade scale.
- **Fahrenheit scale:** A temperature scale that has 180 degrees between the freezing point of water (32°F) and the boiling point of water (212°F).

Because mercury is a highly toxic element, many countries have banned mercury-in-glass thermometers for medical use. Instead, patients' temperatures are now taken using digital thermometers with liquid crystal displays (LCD), like the one shown below.

TYPES OF THERMOMETER

A liquid-in-glass thermometer relates temperature to the movement of a column of liquid expanding in a narrow glass tube. A thermocouple thermometer uses the fact that two junctions between different metals held at different temperatures produce an electric voltage. In a platinum resistance thermometer, temperature is measured in terms of the electrical resistance of a platinum wire coil. A digital thermometer gives a direct reading of temperature.

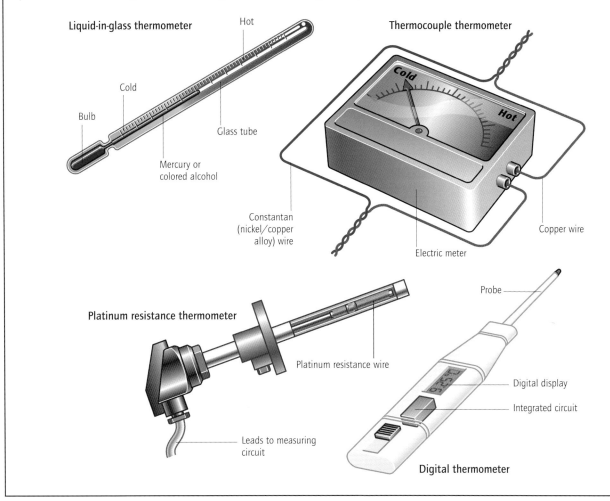

Liquid-in-glass thermometer
Hot
Cold
Bulb
Glass tube
Mercury or colored alcohol

Thermocouple thermometer
Cold
Hot
Constantan (nickel/copper alloy) wire
Electric meter
Copper wire

Platinum resistance thermometer
Platinum resistance wire
Leads to measuring circuit

Probe
Digital display
Integrated circuit
Digital thermometer

A clinical thermometer is a special type used for taking a person's temperature. It works over only a narrow range, usually 95 to 108°F (35 to 42°C). A person's "normal" body temperature is 98.6°F (37°C). There is a narrow kink in the tube situated just above the bulb, so that when the thermometer is removed from the person's mouth, the mercury thread in the tube breaks at the kink. This leaves the upper end of the thread in position, so that the thermometer can be read. The mercury thread has to be shaken back into the bulb before the thermometer is used again. Because mercury is a highly toxic element, many countries have banned mercury-in-glass thermometers for medical use.

Because mercury freezes into a solid at a temperature of –38°F (–38.9°C), a mercury thermometer cannot be used below this temperature. But alcohol does not freeze until the temperate drops to –179°F (–117.3°C), and so it is suitable for low-temperature thermometers.

Expanding metals

Liquid-in-glass thermometers make use of the expansion of liquids when they are heated. Metals also expand slightly when heated, but it is hard to make a mechanism that responds to the slight movement that results. The answer is to use a bimetallic strip—two different metals bonded together. Steel and brass are often used because their expansions are very different. When such a strip is heated, the brass expands more than the steel. This causes the strip to bend, and such movement is made use of in some thermostats, which are devices that maintain a constant temperature by controlling the flow of fuel or electricity to a heater.

In this type of thermometer, the bimetallic strip is a spiral that is fixed at one end. When the strip is heated, the spiral unwinds slightly. The movement is enough to move a pointer across a scale calibrated in degrees.

Other types of thermometer

In theory, any physical property that alters with a change in temperature can be used to make a thermometer. For example, in a thermocouple thermometer a junction between a pair of wires made from different metals is kept at a different temperature from another similar junction. This produces a small electric voltage in the wires. The voltage is measured with a sensitive voltmeter calibrated directly in degrees

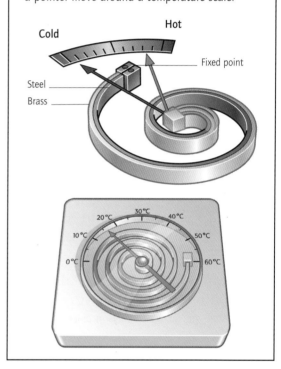

TWO-METAL SPIRAL

In this thermometer, strips of steel and brass are bonded together to form a bimetallic strip. The strip is wound into a coil and fixed at one end. As the temperature rises, the brass expands more than the steel, and the strip uncoils slightly, making a pointer move around a temperature scale.

to give a measure of temperature. Another electrical type is the platinum resistance thermometer. It contains a circuit that measures the change in electrical resistance of a platinum wire as its temperature changes. The resistance can then be matched to the actual temperature.

Temperature conversions

It is sometimes necessary to convert Celsius temperatures to Fahrenheit ones, or the other way

A thermostatic radiator valve controls the flow of hot water to radiators. It has a valve that opens and closes to control the hot water flow and a sensor that controls the opening of the valve.

SCIENCE WORDS

- **Thermocouple:** Temperature-measuring device comprising two wires of different metals joined at their ends. When the joins are at different temperatures, an electric current flows in the wires and can be measured with a sensitive voltmeter, which displays the temperature difference between the joins.
- **Thermostat:** A device for keeping a constant temperature, consisting of a temperature-sensitive element that controls the electricity or fuel supply to a heater.

MAXIMUM AND MINIMUM

This type of thermometer, used for weather records, shows the highest and lowest temperatures over a period. As the temperature rises, the alcohol in the right-hand bulb expands and the mercury rises in the left-hand tube. The mercury pushes a sprung steel marker, which stays in place when the temperature falls and the alcohol contracts. The mercury then rises in the right-hand tube, pushing a second marker. In this way, the markers show the maximum and minimum temperatures.

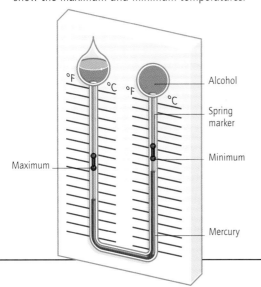

HIGH TEMPERATURES

Very high temperatures, such as those in a furnace, are measured using a pyrometer. In this type, the electric current flowing through a wire filament is adjusted until it has the same brightness as the furnace as viewed through the eyepiece. The meter measures the current, but is marked in degrees.

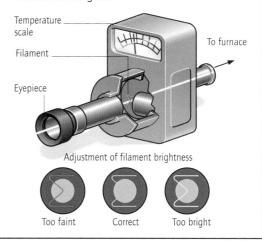

Adjustment of filament brightness
Too faint   Correct   Too bright

around—Fahrenheit to Celsius. This involves a little simple math. To change Celsius to Fahrenheit, multiply by 9 and divide by 5 (or just multiply once by 1.8), then add 32. For example, to convert 50°C to Fahrenheit:

$$\frac{50 * 9}{5} = 90, \quad 90 + 32 = 122°F$$

To convert Fahrenheit to Celsius, we reverse the procedure. First subtract 32, then multiply the result by 5, and divide by 9 (or just multiply once by 0.56). For example, to convert 86°F to Celsius:

$$86 - 32 = 54, \quad \frac{54 * 5}{9} = 30°C$$

Conversion of Celsius to Kelvin is easy—just add 273. For Kelvin to Celsius, subtract 273. Conversion of Fahrenheit to Kelvin is a nuisance. You first have to convert from Fahrenheit to Celsius and then add 273. Reverse the process for converting Kelvin to Fahrenheit.

All the matter around you is made up of atoms—particles so small that about 100 million atoms can span your fingernail. There are some 5,000 trillion trillion atoms in your body. Yet in 1897, the English physicist J. J. Thomson found that atoms contain even smaller particles, later called electrons.

Electrons have negative electric charge. There also has to be positive charge in the atom to balance these negative charges. Thomson suggested that the electrons were embedded in a globe of positive electricity, like raisins in a plum pudding. But then, Ernest Rutherford (1871–1937), a New Zealander, found that the atom's positive charge, and most of its mass, lies at its center in a core called the nucleus. The atom is held together by the electrical attraction of the positive nucleus for the negative electrons.

Into the nucleus

Later experimenters found that the nucleus is itself made up of particles, or nucleons. They are of two types. One is the proton, which has an electric charge

EARLY MODELS OF THE ATOM

Early theorists, such as John Dalton (1766–1844), regarded the atom as having no structure. J. J. Thomson (1856–1940) found that it contained negatively charged electrons. Rutherford showed that the balancing positive charge was concentrated in a nucleus, and Niels Bohr (1885–1962) calculated the sizes of the electrons' orbits.

Thomson: "Plum pudding" 1897   Nucleus   Bohr: "Fixed orbits" 1913

Dalton: "Billiard ball" 1802   Electron   Rutherford: "Electron cloud" 1911

A massive star explodes as a supernova (seen just above center), scattering the elements, visible as rings, "cooked" in its core. They may become the building materials of new stars and their planets.

BUILDING THE ELEMENTS

The simplest atomic nucleus is that of hydrogen, a single positively charged proton. Atoms of other elements contain more protons, with uncharged neutrons to hold them together. The number of protons is called the atomic number (here in brackets). Usually the protons' positive charge is balanced by an equal number of orbiting electrons.

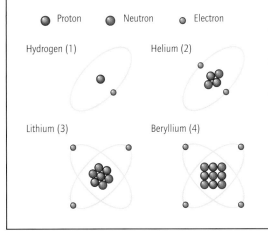

equal but opposite to that of the electron. The mass of the proton is nearly 2,000 times as great as that of the electron. The other type of nucleon is electrically neutral (uncharged) and so is called the neutron. Its mass is approximately equal to that of the proton.

Protons, neutrons, and electrons were built up into atoms in the first few minutes of the Universe, in the fireball of the Big Bang, some 15 billion years ago. But only the simplest and lightest atoms were formed then. Since then, light atoms have been welded together in the centers of stars to make more complex atoms. That is where the carbon, oxygen, nitrogen, and other atoms in your body originated. If a star explodes as a supernova, these and heavier atoms are spread through interstellar space.

Atoms and isotopes

Atoms that behave the same way when they take part in chemical reactions can turn out to be different. The reason lies in the nucleus: Although their nuclei all have the same number of protons, they may have different numbers of neutrons.

There are about 90 kinds of naturally occurring, chemically different atoms on the Earth. They behave very differently in chemical reactions—some react strongly; some react scarcely at all. All these differences are a result of the activity of electrons in the outer parts of the atoms. Atoms join and separate as they gain, lose, or share electrons. The behavior of the atoms depends on the number of electrons in the atoms that are reacting, and that depends on the atom's nucleus.

In ordinary conditions, the number of electrons in an atom equals the number of protons in the nucleus, so that the atom is uncharged overall. This number is called the atomic number, and it is what defines an element. Fluorine has nine electrons and it has that number because there are nine protons in its nucleus. But it has a strong tendency to gain an extra electron because 10 electrons make a very stable system—that is, one that is not easily changed. So fluorine reacts strongly with other atoms from which it can gain an

Niels Bohr

Danish physicist Niels Bohr, born in 1885, provided the first clues to the structure of the atom. He assumed the electrons circled the nucleus like planets orbiting the Sun. A major problem was that, according to the theory then existing, whirling electrons should radiate all their energy in a burst of electromagnetic radiation and fall into the nucleus in a fraction of a second. Bohr could not explain why this did not happen, but went ahead and assumed the electrons stayed in fixed orbits. He was able to calculate their size and energy for the simplest atom, hydrogen. Bohr received the Nobel Prize for Physics in 1922. He played a large part in developing quantum theory, which deals with the physics of the very small, and which has replaced his simple model of the atom with a more complex one. Bohr died in 1962.

SCIENCE WORDS

- **Atomic number:** The number of protons in an element's nucleus. It equals the number of electrons in the normal atom and is the element's numerical position in the periodic table.
- **Isotope:** Any of the varieties of a chemical element that are chemically identical to one another, but whose atoms differ in their relative atomic mass. The atoms of the isotopes of a particular element have the same number of protons in the nucleus and the same number of electrons surrounding the nucleus, but they have different numbers of neutrons in the nucleus.

NAMING ISOTOPES

The two rare isotopes of hydrogen have their own names, deuterium and tritium. They have one or two neutrons, respectively. Most isotopes, like the two carbon isotopes shown here, have no special name. They are identified by the name of the element combined with the mass number, which is the number of protons and neutrons in the nucleus.

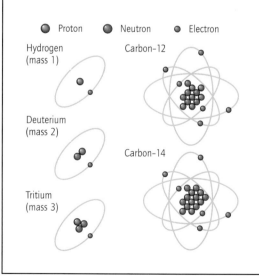

electron. It reacts especially strongly with sodium, which has 11 electrons, and which "tries" to shed one of them to leave just 10 electrons. A sodium and a fluorine atom join together, and an electron is transferred from the sodium to the fluorine, giving out energy in the form of heat.

But two atoms can have the same atomic number and yet differ in important ways. Although they have the same number of protons in the nucleus and are therefore chemically identical, they can have different numbers of neutrons. Ordinary hydrogen has a nucleus consisting of one proton and no neutrons. A rarer form has one proton joined to one neutron in the nucleus

and is called deuterium. A still rarer form has one proton and two neutrons in the nucleus, and is known as tritium.

Exploring isotopes

These different forms of an element are called isotopes of that element. They were first discovered by J. J. Thomson, discoverer of the electron, who found two varieties of the gas neon. His student Francis Aston (1877–1945) studied isotopes thoroughly when he made very accurate measurements of the masses of atoms from 1919 onward. Aston formed beams of fast-moving ions. Ions are atoms that have lost or gained

---

TRY THIS

Making heavy water

Deuterium is the isotope of hydrogen with a neutron, as well as a proton in its nucleus. Oxygen combines chemically with hydrogen to form water (H_2O). When oxygen combines with deuterium, the combination is called heavy water (D_2O). It is called heavy water because deuterium was originally known as heavy hydrogen. All natural water contains a tiny fraction of heavy water (0.003 percent). In this project, we will increase the amount of heavy water in a sample of ordinary water.

What to do

Nearly fill a glass jar or beaker with water, and add five teaspoonfuls of vinegar. Wrap one end of each of two wires around the terminals of a battery. Connect alligator clips on the other ends of the wire to the ends of two very thick pencil leads. Dip the leads into the watery vinegar (making sure they do not touch). Leave the setup for a while.

If you look carefully, you will see small bubbles of gas on the pencil leads. On the lead connected to the positive (+) terminal of the battery the gas is oxygen. On the lead connected to the negative (–) terminal of the battery it is flammable hydrogen. The current is decomposing the water

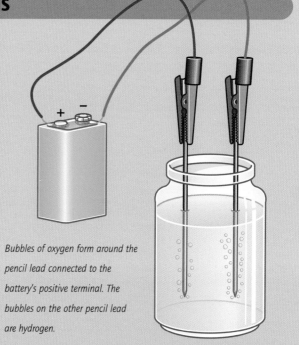

Bubbles of oxygen form around the pencil lead connected to the battery's positive terminal. The bubbles on the other pencil lead are hydrogen.

into its component elements, oxygen and hydrogen (in a process called electrolysis). There is also some heavy water in the vinegar solution, but it is not so easily broken down by electrolysis as normal water is. As you leave the experiment running, the concentration of heavy water very gradually increases. The same process has been used on a large scale for making heavy water for some kinds of nuclear reactor.

one or more electrons to form electrically charged particles. They can be accelerated by passing them through an electric field. Magnetic fields have the effect of bending the paths of these electrically charged particles.

Aston passed his ion beams through both electric and magnetic fields, and was able to separate them into beams depending on the charge and mass of the ions. He called his device a mass spectrometer because it spread out the beams of ions in much the same way as an optical spectrometer spreads out a beam of light. Closely related devices are called mass spectroscopes and mass spectrographs.

Such experiments show that, for example, chlorine atoms are of two main types. Approximately three-fourths has a mass 35 times that of the hydrogen atom; the other fourth has a mass 37 times that of the hydrogen atom. This explained why chemists had already found that the mass of the chlorine atom is 35.45 times that of hydrogen: they had been measuring an average.

The mass of an atom is expressed as its relative atomic mass, or r.a.m. The r.a.m. of the most common isotope of carbon, with six protons and six neutrons, is defined to be exactly equal to 12; on this scale the r.a.m. of hydrogen is 1.008.

TRY THIS

Isotopes and decay

Some atoms form isotopes, which have an abnormal number of neutrons in their nuclei. And some isotopes are unstable. They become stable again by ejecting particles from their nuclei in a process known as decay. In this project, you will make models of some simple isotopes and then look at a typical decay process.

What to do

Roll some balls of modeling clay to represent protons (in red clay, say) and neutrons (in blue clay, say). First, make models of the nuclei of the three isotopes of hydrogen, which are normal hydrogen (H), deuterium (D), and tritium (T). They are very simple: the normal hydrogen nucleus has just one proton, deuterium's nucleus has one proton and one neutron, and the nucleus of tritium has one proton and two neutrons. Notice that deuterium is twice the size (and weight) of normal hydrogen, and tritium is three times the size (and weight).

Normal carbon has 12 particles in its nucleus (six protons and six neutrons), and it is also known as carbon-12. But carbon has an isotope, called carbon-14, with 14 particles in its nucleus. There are still six protons, but there are two extra

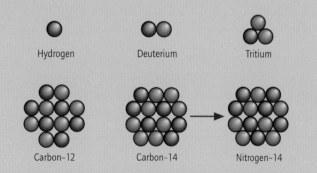

The top row shows models of the three isotopes of hydrogen. The first and second models in the second row are the two isotopes of carbon, called carbon-12 and carbon-14. Carbon-14 is radioactive and decays to form nitrogen-14, the ordinary nonradioactive form of nitrogen.

neutrons, bringing their total to eight. Make a model of this nucleus from balls of modeling clay. Carbon-14 is unstable and radioactive. It becomes more stable when one of the neutrons in its nucleus changes into a proton; that is called radioactive decay. To model this event, remove one blue ball, and replace it with a red one. Do you recognize the new nucleus you have just made? It is a nitrogen atom (with seven protons and seven neutrons).

SCIENCE WORDS

- **Ion:** An atom or molecule that has lost or gained one or more electrons, so gaining an electric charge.
- **Mass spectrograph:** An instrument that separates fast-moving ions in a beam according to their mass. Similar devices are the mass spectrometer and the mass spectroscope.
- **Relative atomic mass:** The mass of an atom expressed in atomic mass units (amu). The atomic mass unit is defined as one-twelfth of the mass of the common isotope of carbon and is approximately equal to the mass of the hydrogen atom.

THE MASS SPECTROGRAPH

The collimating slits let through a narrow beam of ions. The combination of the electric field and the magnetic field causes ions of different mass to move in curves of different radius, striking the photographic plate at different positions.

Ion source

Collimating slits

Electric field

Photographic plate

+   −

Magnetic field at right angles to ion beams

Paths of positive ions

Stability and instability

There must be at least as many neutrons as protons to make a stable nucleus—that is, one that will last unchanged. If there are too few or too many neutrons, the nucleus will disintegrate, or break down. It will do this by giving out particles or breaking in two to form other nuclei. That can happen repeatedly until stable nuclei are formed. The breaking down of a nucleus, transforming it into others, is called radioactivity. (Another type of radioactivity involves just giving out energy in the form of radiation, without changing the identity of the nucleus.)

In nuclei of low atomic number, there can be stable nuclei with equal numbers of neutrons and protons, as in the cases of carbon (atomic number 6), oxygen (atomic number 8), and calcium (atomic number 20). But because all protons have positive electrical charge, they tend to repel one another. As a result, heavier nuclei need extra neutrons to hold the nucleus together against the force of repulsion between

Francis Aston

Francis Aston (1877–1945) gained the first clue to the existence of isotopes when working with J. J. Thomson at Cambridge in 1913, but further study was interrupted by World War I (1914–18). In 1919, Aston built a much improved version of the equipment he had previously used. The device revealed that atoms that were chemically identical could have slightly different masses. Nearly every element studied was found to have several isotopes. Aston announced the whole-number rule, which states that the masses of isotopes are whole-number multiples of the mass of the hydrogen atom. He also discovered the rule of odd and even: elements of odd-numbered relative atomic mass (r.a.m.) usually have isotopes of odd-numbered r.a.m., and those of even r.a.m. usually have isotopes of even r.a.m. Aston spent the rest of his career building ever more accurate mass spectrometers.

the many protons. The most stable isotope of uranium, atomic number 92, has 146 neutrons, but even so it is weakly radioactive.

Separating isotopes

Separating isotopes can be very difficult, but the problem had to be solved in World War II in order to build the first nuclear bomb. Now the same technology has countless peaceful uses. Specific isotopes are needed for industrial measurement, medical diagnosis, and biological study.

Once scientists had discovered the existence of isotopes, they had to separate them in order to study them. That was not easy to do because the isotopes of an element are chemically identical and so are affected in the same way by a given chemical process.

The principle behind the mass spectrograph was developed for large-scale processes. Substances containing a mixture of isotopes are ionized, and a beam of the ions is passed through electric and

SCIENCE WORDS

- **Calutron:** A large mass spectrometer used for separating the isotopes of uranium.
- **Centrifuge:** A machine with a fast-spinning chamber that creates strong "artificial gravity" to separate materials of different densities. It is used in the enrichment of uranium to make nuclear fuel.
- **Electrolysis:** The decomposition of an electrolyte—a liquid that conducts electricity—by electric current, using two electrodes.
- **Gas diffusion:** A technology used in the enrichment of materials used in nuclear reactors and nuclear weapons.

Shown here is a calutron, a kind of mass spectrometer, designed in the 1940s to separate the isotopes of uranium. With this, nuclear physicists produced quantities of enriched uranium-235.

TWO WAYS OF SEPARATING ISOTOPES

A centrifugal separation unit receives a mixture of gaseous isotopes as "feedstock" and returns one stream of gas that is enriched in the lighter isotope and another that is depleted. At each stage of a gas–diffusion separation plant the depleted part of the output is sent on, while the enriched part is passed back to an earlier stage.

Centrifugal separation

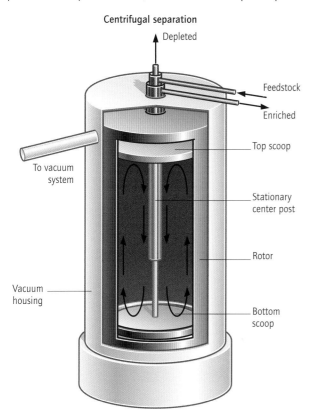

Gas-diffusion separation

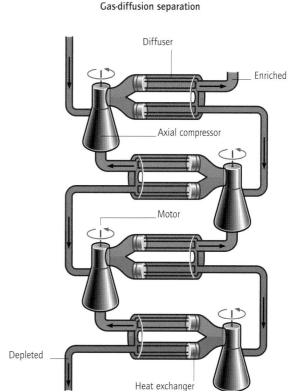

In centrifugal separation, a gaseous mixture of isotopes is passed into a fast-spinning chamber. The heavier isotopes are thrown outward to the edge of the rotating chamber slightly more strongly than are the lighter isotopes, and so there is partial separation. Streams of gas are collected from the center of the centrifuge and the edge of the centrifuge by two "scoops."

In gas-diffusion separation, Uranium is combined with fluorine to make the gas uranium hexafluoride. It is allowed to diffuse through a porous membrane. The uranium-235 moves slightly faster, so the gas emerging is slightly enriched. The gas is put through the same process thousands of times, gradually increasing the proportion of uranium-235. Then electromagnetic separation is used for the final enrichment.

magnetic fields. The beam splits up because the ions that have less mass are more readily deflected.

The first to succeed in separating isotopes on a larger scale was the American chemist Harold Urey (1893-1981), who in 1932 separated the rare isotopes of hydrogen, called deuterium and tritium, from the common isotope. He did it by the electrolysis of water—that is, by breaking down water into hydrogen and oxygen by passing an electric current through it. The hydrogen that is released bubbles off, but the heavier isotopes do so more slowly. So the water left behind is slightly enriched in the rare isotopes.

MASS AND WEIGHT

The mass of an object remains the same wherever it is on the Earth. It even stays the same if we send it to the Moon or launch it by rocket into outer space. But an object's weight can change depending on the local force of gravity.

Mass is a measure of the amount of matter in an object. That is why an object's mass always remains the same, wherever it is. But the weight of an object is the force acting on it by the gravitational attraction of the Earth (or any other nearby planetary body). As a result, an object's weight depends on its distance from the Earth. It is very slightly less at the top of a high mountain than at sea level. On the surface of the Moon the same object would weigh only about one-sixth of its

The NASA space shuttles need powerful rocket motors to lift them into space against the force of Earth's gravity.

weight on Earth. That is because the Moon's force of gravity is only one-sixth of the Earth's.

The scientific unit of mass is the kilogram (kg); the unit of weight is the newton (N). An object's weight is equal to its mass multiplied by the acceleration due to gravity (which is also called the acceleration of free fall). Because this equals 9.8 meters per second per second ($9.8 \ m/s^2$) at the surface of the Earth, there is a simple relationship between weight (in newtons) and mass (in kilograms):

weight = 9.8 * mass

Thus a person whose mass is 50 kg weighs 490 newtons. The same person would weigh only 82 N on the Moon—and a huge 1,294 N on the giant planet Jupiter!

TRY THIS

Do heavy things fall faster than light things?
Which falls faster—an iron cannonball or a feather? The famous Italian scientist Galileo is supposed to have dropped things from the top of the Leaning Tower of Pisa to find out. You can try it with a coin and a paper disk.

What to do
Cut a disk of paper very slightly smaller than a coin. With your arms stretched out sideways and hands palms down, hold the disk horizontally with the fingers of one hand around its edge. Do the same with the coin in the other hand. Drop them at the same time. Which hits the ground first?

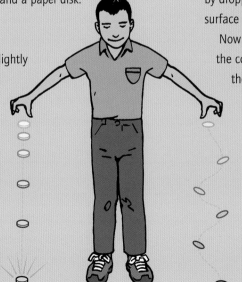

The paper falls more slowly, but not because it is lighter than the coin. It is slowed down by air resistance and "floats" on the air as it falls. If there were no air, the two objects would fall at the same rate. A NASA astronaut proved this by dropping a hammer and a feather onto the airless surface of the Moon. They hit the ground at the same time. Now put the paper on top of the coin and, holding just the coin by its edges, without touching the paper, drop the two together. This time the paper travels with the coin and hits the ground at the same time. Air pressure above the coin keeps the paper in place, so that the paper hitches a ride with the falling coin.

You can repeat the experiment on a larger scale using an old book and a sheet of paper. Cut a rectangle of paper slightly smaller than the book, lay it flat on the book's cover, and drop them both together.

Try to drop the coin and the paper disk at exactly the same time.

Everyday weight

Scientists are always very careful to distinguish between mass and weight. But this difference is not so important in everyday life. In fact, for ordinary measurements we tend to use mass units to express weights. Thus we say that a person weighs 50 kg, and buys 5 kg of potatoes.

Sometimes we need to convert from one system of mass/weight to another. To convert from kilograms to pounds, multiply by 2.2 (thus 50 kg = 110 lb). To convert the other way, from pounds to kilograms, divide by 2.2.

Machines for weighing

The earliest weighing machines—balances—are still used throughout science and industry. They consist of

SCIENCE WORDS

- **Acceleration:** The rate of change in a moving object's velocity. It is a vector quantity.
- **newton:** (N) The derived SI unit of force. It is the force required to give a mass of 1 kilogram an acceleration of 1 meter per second per second.
- **Weight:** The force with which a mass is drawn toward the Earth (by the force of gravity).

SLOWING DOWN GRAVITY

To study a falling ball, Galileo slowed it down by rolling it along a slope. He measured how far the ball rolled in equal time intervals and found that speed increased uniformly with time.

0 1 2 3 4 5

Equal time intervals

0 2 4 6 8 10 12 14 16 18 20 22 24 26 28   Distance

MASS AND WEIGHT

a horizontal beam pivoted at its center so that it balances—hence the name! A pan hangs from each end of the beam. To weigh out a particular quantity, say a kilogram of rice, a mass of 1 kilogram is put on one pan. Rice is then poured onto the other pan until the beam is again horizontal—until it balances. To find the weight of a particular quantity, it is put in one pan, and known weights are added to the other pan until it balances. So to use the device for weighing things you need a set of known weights.

Of course, such a "weighing" exercise as this doesn't really find the weight of anything: what it does is to

SCIENCE WORDS

- **Center of gravity:** Also called center of mass, the point at which an object's total mass appears to be concentrated and at which it acts.
- **Force:** An influence that changes the shape, position, or movement of an object.

GRAVITY AND LIGHT

A gravitational field can bend a beam of light. When light from a distant object passes on either side of a galaxy, the galaxy's powerful gravity bends the light rays. An observer on Earth sees two images of the same object, one on each side of the galaxy. (This diagram is not to scale.)

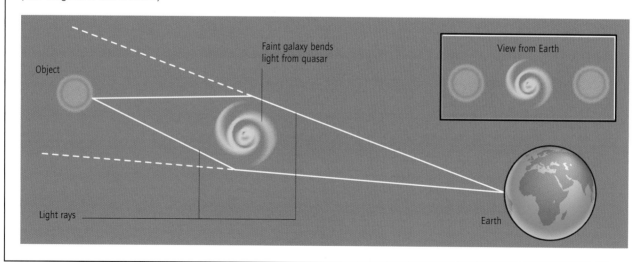

Object

Faint galaxy bends light from quasar

View from Earth

Light rays

Earth

A weightlifter strains to lift heavy weights against the force of the Earth's gravity. He would find it much easier if he tried it on the Moon!

manipulate masses. This type of balance would work just as well on the Moon because it actually compares masses. But a spring balance is different. Most mechanical kitchen scales are of this type, with a vertical coiled spring and a pan on top that compresses the spring. A pointer that is worked by the movement of the spring indicates weights on a marked dial. This device measures the effect of the force of gravity on an object's mass. It is therefore a force meter; similar devices used in physics laboratories are called newton-meters. The spring balance measures weight and would register only a sixth of an object's "Earth weight" if the same object were weighed with it on the Moon.

Force of gravity

Every object is attracted toward every other object by a force known as gravitation, which arises because objects have mass. The force of gravity is simply the force of attraction between an object and the much more massive Earth. When you drop something, it is this force that makes it fall to the ground. The actual

Galileo

Galileo Galilei (1564-1632), to give him his full name, was an astronomer and physicist who was born in Pisa, Italy. One of his main subjects of study was gravity. Observing the swinging lamps in Pisa cathedral, he realized that the regular swinging motion of a pendulum might be used to regulate a clock. He studied falling objects by dropping weights from towers and rolling balls down inclined planes. Galileo also made one of the first telescopes, which he used to discover craters on the Moon, sunspots, and the four moons of Jupiter. He also backed Copernicus (1473-1543) by saying that the Earth orbits the Sun, and not the other way around, as was then believed.

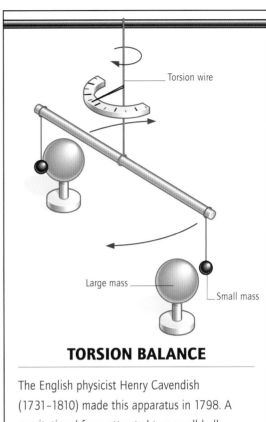

TORSION BALANCE

The English physicist Henry Cavendish (1731-1810) made this apparatus in 1798. A gravitational force attracted two small balls toward two larger ones, causing twisting in the suspension. From the amount of twisting, he calculated the value of the gravitational constant.

size of the force between any two objects depends on their masses and their distance apart. In mathematical terms, we say the force is proportional to the product of the masses divided by the square of the distance between them. As a result, the closer they are together, the stronger is the force of attraction between them. If the masses are m_1 and m_2, and the distance between them is d, the force F between them can be expressed as

$$F = G \frac{m_1 * m_2}{d^2}$$

where G is the gravitational constant. This equation is an example of an inverse square law, so called because the strength of some quantity (here, force) gets less with the square of the distance from a particular point.

FALLING OBJECTS

When an object falls under the force of gravity, does it fall at a constant speed, or does it get faster and faster? In other words, does it accelerate? This question puzzled early scientists until Galileo did some experiments to find the answer.

ACCELERATION DUE TO GRAVITY

The figures show how an object would fall in the first 3 seconds after being dropped from the Leaning Tower of Pisa. Its speed increases, but its acceleration is constant at 32 ft/s² (9.8 m/s²).

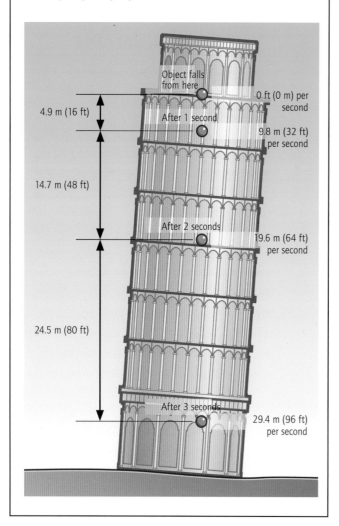

4.9 m (16 ft)

14.7 m (48 ft)

24.5 m (80 ft)

Object falls from here — 0 ft (0 m) per second

After 1 second — 9.8 m (32 ft) per second

After 2 seconds — 19.6 m (64 ft) per second

After 3 seconds — 29.4 m (96 ft) per second

Galileo's experiment illustrated on page 21 shows how he found that the speed of a ball rolling down a slope continues to increase—in other words, it accelerates. Galileo also found that every freely falling object has the same acceleration. Now called the acceleration due to gravity, it has the value 32 ft/s² (9.8 m/s²).

According to tradition, Galileo also tried to measure the acceleration of a cannonball dropped off the top of the Leaning Tower of Pisa. The illustration on the

movement of the object, and this air resistance acts as an upward force called drag. The drag increases as the object's speed increases so that eventually the object can go no faster. Most falling objects reach a constant terminal speed of about 177 ft/s (about 120 mph; 54 m/s). Think of the damage hailstones could do if they fell any faster!

Drag is larger on an object with a large area than it is on one with a small area. This is the principle of a parachute, which when open gives a falling human a terminal speed of nearly 21 ft/s (14 mph; 6.3 m/s). That is the speed at which a parachutist hits the ground. You can prove the principle with a sheet of paper. Drop it, and it flutters to the ground because of the high drag acting on it. But crumple it into a tight ball, and you will find that it falls much quicker because there is much less drag.

Free fall

An object falling under the force of gravity is said to be in free fall (and acceleration due to gravity is also known as acceleration of free fall). It has the symbol g, and crops up in many of the physical formulas that have to do with mechanics, such as the formula for calculating the time of a pendulum's swing and equations for calculating pressures under water.

left shows what the results would have been if he had had a way of making such measurements (which he did not). The cannonball would have reached a speed of 32 ft/s (9.8 m/s) after 1 second, a speed of 64 ft/s (19.6 m/s) after 2 seconds, and so on. The speed increases, but the acceleration is unchanging.

Terminal speed

In practice, an object falling in air does not keep getting faster and faster. The air resists the downward

SCIENCE WORDS

- **Air resistance:** A force, also called drag or wind resistance, that resists the movement of an object through the air. It is overcome by streamlining.
- **Terminal speed:** The maximum speed at which an object falls under the influence of gravity.

VECTORS AND SCALARS

Most quantities in physics are expressed as a number and some unit, such as 25 kg or 110 volts. These last examples are called scalars. But what is the difference between a speed of 50 km/h and a velocity of 50 km/h in the direction of Chicago? The first (speed) is a scalar, but the second (velocity) is a vector quantity.

A vector quantity always has its direction specified, whereas a scalar is a pure number. A given quantity can be either, and sometimes the difference is very important. If you told some shipwrecked sailors on a life raft that there was an island only 3 miles away, they might be relieved. But it would be much more useful for them to know that there was an island 3 miles away to the north. They would then know which way to paddle the life raft. We call "3 miles away" a

SCIENCE WORDS

- **Scalar:** A quantity that has magnitude but (unlike a vector) no specified direction. Examples of scalars are speed and mass.
- **Triangle of vectors:** A way of adding vectors. The first vector is drawn as a line at the correct angle, with the length of the line representing its magnitude. The second vector is drawn from the end of the first line, again at the correct angle and of the correct length. A third line joining the beginning of the first line to the end of the second line (completing the triangle) gives the magnitude and direction of the sum of the vectors.

Air-traffic controllers use vectors to indicate the position of airplanes. They need to know how far away the airplanes are and in what direction. Often the vectors are plotted on a radar screen.

scalar quantity; "3 miles away to the north" is a vector. Several quantities in physics are vectors. They include velocity, acceleration, and most forces.

Adding vectors

Adding scalar quantities is easy as long as you can do simple math. A piece of string 3 feet long added to a piece 4 feet long gives a total length of 7 feet of string (ignoring the string used to tie the knot).

But adding vectors is trickier. If you push a cart 30 feet to the east and then 40 feet to the south, where does the cart end up? The answer is 50 feet away from where you started, in a more or less south-easterly direction. Notice that the cart does not finish up 70

feet away, which is the result you would get if you merely added the two distances. The math is a bit more complicated this time.

Drawing conclusions

One way of adding vectors is to draw a plan. Make the length of a line stand for the size of the vector, and draw it in the correct direction. Then, from the end of the first line draw a second line in the direction of the second vector, again with length standing for size. A line drawn between the beginning of the first line and the end of the second one represents the sum of the vectors and its direction. The construction you have made is called a triangle of vectors.

TRIANGLES AND PARALLELOGRAMS

The triangle of vectors (right) shows how to add vectors, in this case two forces. The effect of combining a force F_1 in one direction and another force F_2 in a different direction (the lengths of the arrows indicate the sizes of the forces) is called the resultant. The third side of the triangle shows the resultant's size and direction.

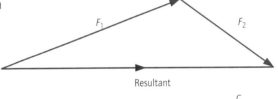

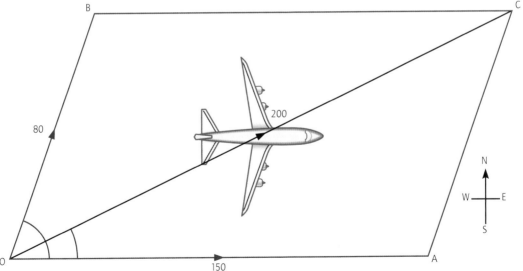

Problem: an airplane navigator wants to fly a plane 200 miles from O to C. But there is a northerly wind along the line from O to B. What course should the navigator set? The correct course is due east, toward A. The parallelogram of vectors shows that the plane will actually fly along the line from O to C, as required.

FORCE AND ACCELERATION

Force is what makes a thing move or stops it. The ease with which something moves depends on its mass. A moving object has a certain speed, and if its speed changes it accelerates. Force, mass, and acceleration are interconnected.

Force can make things move, stop moving, move faster or slower, or change the direction in which they move. It can also make things change shape, perhaps by squeezing them or stretching them. If you stretch a rubber band or snap a pencil you are using force. Even a humble paper clip exerts a force when it holds two pieces of paper together.

All the forces mentioned so far have to do with objects in contact with one another. But there are other forces that act at a distance. As we saw earlier, gravity is a force that pulls things down to the surface of the

Earth. A magnet exerts a force when it picks up an iron nail. There are also forces that act between electric charges. In fact, nearly all of physics is concerned with forces of one sort or another. But forces are most obvious when they have to do with movement, with what scientists call motion.

The laws of motion

If you roll a ball along the ground, it does not keep on rolling forever, but soon slows down and stops. Have you ever wondered why? In the 17th century, the English scientist Isaac Newton (1642-1727) wondered why and came up with a set of rules that apply to all moving objects. Together, these rules are now known as Newton's laws of motion.

> ### Isaac Newton
>
> Sir Isaac Newton (1642-1727) was an English mathematician, astronomer, and physicist. He was born at Woolsthorpe in Lincolnshire and in 1661 went to study at Cambridge University. In 1669, he became professor of mathematics there. In mathematics, Newton developed calculus, a system that can deal with changing quantities. In astronomy, he made one of the first reflecting telescopes and worked out how the Moon orbits the Earth. To do this, he used the law of gravitation, one of his major contributions to physics. He studied light and produced the Sun's spectrum by passing sunlight through a glass prism. He also formulated his three famous laws of motion. In 1705, he became the first scientist ever to be knighted. He is buried in Westminster Abbey in London and is regarded as one of the world's greatest scientists.

When the hockey player hits the puck, it slides across the ice and, according to Newton's laws, would go on forever if the force of friction did not slow it down.

Reaction

Action

A person firing a rifle demonstrates the third law of motion (see page 30). When the rifle is fired, a force (the action) speeds the bullet forward. At the same time, the shooter feels a sudden recoil (the reaction) as the rifle is pushed backward.

The first law states that an object at rest will stay at rest, or a moving object will go on moving, unless a force acts on it. So according to Newton, our ball started rolling because we gave it a push—we applied a force. It then stopped rolling because it was acted on by another force. In this case, the second force was friction between the ball and the ground. That is why a ball will roll farther on a smooth surface than it will on a rough one—try rolling a marble across a wooden floor (low friction) and across a carpet (high friction).

Newton's second law of motion involves acceleration, which is the rate at which a moving object changes speed. The law says that the force acting on an object is equal to its mass multiplied by its acceleration. So if you give something a push (apply a force), it will move off at a certain speed. But if you want it to move faster and faster, you have to keep on applying force. A spacecraft returning to the Earth from

TRY THIS

Rocket balloon

The gases under pressure inside a rocket push in all directions, but the only way they can escape is through the nozzle at the rear of the rocket. A reaction force pushes in the opposite direction, and it is this force that makes the rocket move forward. In this project, you use reaction to make a balloon into a rocket.

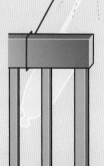

What to do

Cut a drinking straw in half (throw away one half). Thread one end of a piece of string about 12 ft (3.5 m) long through the straw. Place two sturdy chairs about 8 ft (2.5 m) apart, and tie the ends of the string to the chair backs. Move the chairs apart until the string is taut. Cut two short lengths of masking tape, and blow up the balloon. Twist the neck of the balloon to keep in the air. This is where you may need some help. Slide the straw to one end of the string, and tape it onto the inflated balloon. Finally, let go of the neck of the balloon—it will jet along the string under rocket power.

The escape of compressed air powers the rocket balloon along its string.

the Moon travels at a fairly constant speed until it gets close to the Earth. Then the Earth's gravity (a force) has more effect and makes it accelerate. Strictly speaking, we should use the term velocity instead of speed (velocity is speed in a specified direction).

The third law of motion concerns two objects. It states that when one object exerts a force on another, the second object exerts the same force on the first, but in the opposite direction. The first force is an action and the second a reaction, and the law is sometimes stated as "action and reaction are equal and opposite."

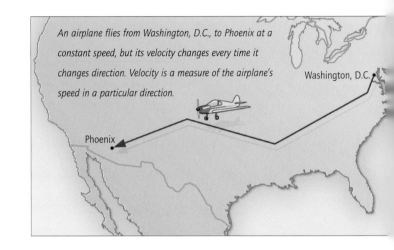

An airplane flies from Washington, D.C., to Phoenix at a constant speed, but its velocity changes every time it changes direction. Velocity is a measure of the airplane's speed in a particular direction.

SCIENCE WORDS

- **Inertia:** The property of an object that makes it tend to resist being moved or, if moving, to resist a change in direction. It is a consequence of the first of Newton's laws of motion.
- **Momentum:** The mass of an object multiplied by its velocity in a straight line.

When we drop a book, gravity is the action force that makes it fall. There is also an equal reaction force between the book and the Earth, but it is undetectable because the mass of the Earth is huge compared with that of the book. The forces between the Earth and the Moon are easier to grasp. The Earth's gravity pulls on the Moon and keeps it in orbit. The Moon's gravity pulls on the water in the Earth's oceans, causing the daily tides.

Another example of the third law is the principle of the rocket. The hot burning gases in a rocket expand and push in all directions. Those that push on the

STARTING AND STOPPING

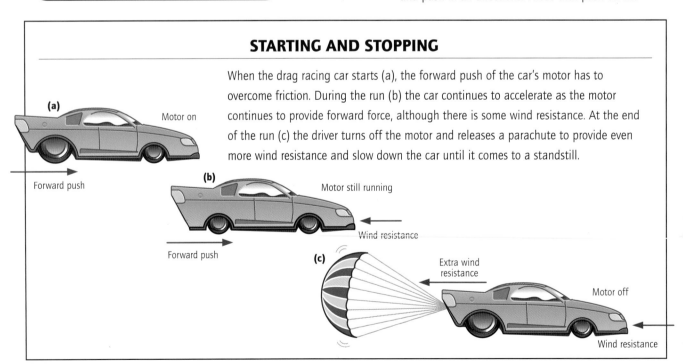

When the drag racing car starts (a), the forward push of the car's motor has to overcome friction. During the run (b) the car continues to accelerate as the motor continues to provide forward force, although there is some wind resistance. At the end of the run (c) the driver turns off the motor and releases a parachute to provide even more wind resistance and slow down the car until it comes to a standstill.

closed front end of the rocket are balanced by a reaction, which acts in the opposite direction and propels the rocket along. For this reason, a rocket is known technically as a type of reaction motor.

Inertia and momentum

A heavy object is more difficult to start moving than a lighter one. That is because of its mass or inertia. Inertia can be thought of as an object's reluctance to move. If you are traveling in an automobile and the driver brakes suddenly, it is your inertia that makes you keep moving unless held back by a seat belt.

Once an object is moving, it has momentum, which is equal to its mass multiplied by its velocity. The more massive a moving object is, or the faster it moves, the greater is its momentum.

It is easy to demonstrate the difference between inertia and momentum. If you carefully place a brick on your foot, it is difficult to raise your toes—that's inertia. But if you dropped the brick on your foot, it would do a lot of damage—that's momentum! A small object moving very fast can have more momentum than a massive object moving slowly. For example, a bullet fired from a Magnum revolver can have enough momentum to stop a moving automobile because the bullet's momentum is greater than that of the car.

Newton's second and third laws of motion predict that when two objects bump into each other, their total momentum after impact is the same as it was before impact. This statement is often called the principle of conservation of momentum. It explains various things in everyday life, particularly in sports. People playing pool or hockey make unconscious use of the conservation of momentum when they strike a ball or the puck.

Like velocity, acceleration is a vector quantity. It is specified by a number (how large it is) and a direction. An example of a velocity is "5 feet per second northward." Acceleration is measured in units such as meters per second per second. Speed, on the other hand, is a scalar quantity. It is stated just as a number and unit with no direction, such as "500 mph."

TRY THIS

Check that checker

This project relies on inertia. The idea is to remove the bottom checker from a stack of checkers without touching it or knocking over the stack. As with many such demonstrations, there is a trick to it.

What to do

Stack nine of the checkers in a neat pile on a shiny surface. Place the tenth checker about 1 inch (2.5 cm) away from the bottom of the stack. With your finger and thumb flick the single checker hard against the base of the stack. The bottom checker will shoot off sideways, leaving the rest of the stack in place. (Some people will find it easier to use the edge of a ruler to flick the bottom checker away.)

Inertia is the reluctance of a stationary object to move. It is inertia that keeps the other checkers from moving even when the bottom one is forced violently sideways. If you master the trick of using a ruler to strike the checker, you can knock out any of the checkers in the stack—not just the bottom one—without disturbing the others.

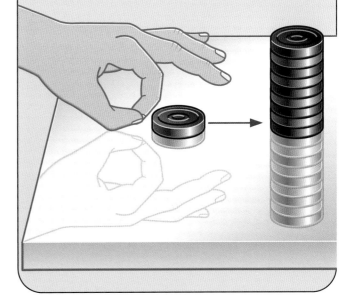

Flick the single checker hard at the base of the pile (or hit it with the edge of a ruler).

MOTION IN A CIRCLE

So far we have considered mainly objects moving in straight lines and the various forces that can act on them. Slightly different rules apply if an object is moving in a curved path, particularly if it is moving around and around in a circle.

We are going to begin with a very difficult idea. When an object moves in a straight line, the only way it can accelerate (or decelerate) is by changing its speed—by going faster (or slower). But we know from pages 26 to 27 that velocity is a vector quantity. So if an object is moving at a certain speed in a certain direction (that is, if it has a certain velocity), it can be acted on by a force—for example, by giving it a sideways push—that changes its direction without changing its speed. As a result, its velocity changes. And that amounts to saying that it undergoes acceleration, which after all is defined as change in velocity divided by time. So, although it might seem unlikely at first, it is quite possible for something to be accelerating without its speed changing.

Now think of a stone tied to the end of a piece of string and whirled around your head in a horizontal circle. Its speed is constant; but because its direction is continuously changing, it is always accelerating. The force that accelerates the stone is the pull in the string. Its direction is at right angles to the direction of the stone at any instant, directed inward toward the center of the circle. Physicists call it centripetal force.

FEEDBACK CONTROL

A mechanism for controlling the speed of an engine, called a governor, makes use of circular motion. The vertical shaft is turned by a belt (1) driven by the machine. As it turns, the weights (2), attached at the top of the shaft, go around and rise (3). This action raises the rod (4), which reduces the power supply to the engine and slows it down. As it slows, the weights fall and so increase the power to the engine.

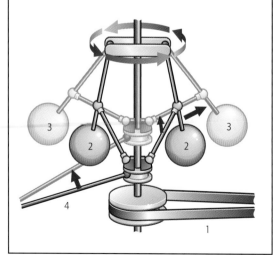

People on this carnival ride feel as though they are being flung outward. In fact, their velocity constantly changes as they go around in a circle.

TRY THIS

Spinning water

When objects spin around fast in a circle, there is a force trying to push them in toward the center. It is called centripetal force and is the principle behind a spin drier. The drier makes the wet laundry go around in a circle, but the water moves outward through the holes in the spinning drum, like a hammer thrower's hammer when the athlete lets go of it. This project demonstrates centripetal force.

What to do

Pour water into a large mixing bowl until the water is about 4 in (10 cm) deep. Float a cereal bowl on the water, and then pour a little water into the cereal bowl until the water is about ¼ in (1 cm) deep. Place the brush of a dish brush in the cereal bowl, and use it to spin the cereal bowl around (or use your index finger if you have no dish brush). Keep spinning until the cereal bowl is going really fast.

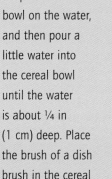

Spin the small bowl around and around, and watch the water in it rise.

The water in the spinning bowl will move toward the edge of the bowl and "crawl" up the sides until the bottom of the bowl is dry. As the bowl slows down, the water will sink back toward the center and again cover the bottom. The water has behaved like the water in a spin drier.

Moons and satellites

Isaac Newton (1642–1727) worked out that a force is involved in keeping an object moving in a circle around another object. So what keeps the Moon orbiting the Earth? It is the force of gravity between the Earth and the Moon. In a way, the Moon is always falling in a circle toward the Earth. But it keeps falling past and going around again—or at least it has for the last 4½ billion years or so!

Artificial satellites orbiting any planet act in the same way under the gravitational attraction of the body that they orbit. To lift an orbiting satellite into a higher orbit, it has to be given more speed (by firing its rocket motors). When a satellite slows down, perhaps because of friction between it and the outer layers of the Earth's atmosphere, it can no longer stay in its orbit and soon spirals down toward the Earth.

HAMMER THROWER

Centripetal force in the chain attached to the hammer produces its acceleration in a circle. When the thrower lets go, the hammer flies off in the direction it was traveling at the instant it was released.

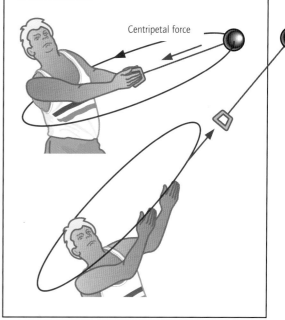

Centripetal force

THE SWINGING PENDULUM

A pendulum swings through an arc of a circle, with the suspension point at the center of the circle. Two quantities that can be varied are the length of the pendulum and the mass of the pendulum bob. Only one of them affects the time of the swing.

There is a traditional story about the first person to observe the perfectly regular swing of a pendulum—one of many anecdotes told about Galileo (1594-1632). In 1602, while sitting in Pisa cathedral, he noticed the ceiling lamps swinging in the breeze. He did not have a watch (they had not yet been invented), so he timed the swings by feeling the pulse in his wrist.

Galileo found that each lamp swung at a regular pace, and that lamps on long chains swung more slowly than on short ones. He also speculated whether heavy lamps swung more slowly than lighter ones. He could not weigh the lamps, so he did some experiments.

In 1851, at the Panthéon in Paris, the French physicist Léon Foucault (1819-1868) conducted a famous experiment using a pendulum to demonstrate the rotation of the Earth.

LENGTH AND MASS

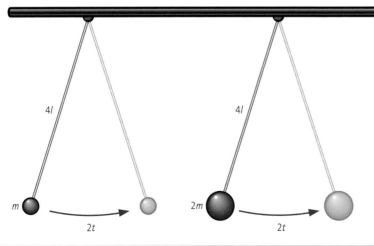

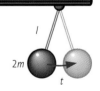

The left-hand pair of pendulums have a cord 4*l* long. The time of the swing is 2*t*, which does not change even when the mass is doubled from *m* to 2*m*. But shortening the cord to *l* (pair above) halves the time of swing to *t*.

The results of Galileo's experiments with pendulums are illustrated at the bottom of page 34. Galileo found that changing the mass of the bob (the weight at the end of the cord) had no effect on the time of the swing as long as the pendulum swung through only small angles. But changing the length of the cord did change the time of the swing. This time period was halved when he shortened the cord to one-fourth of its former length.

Enter gravity

Galileo found that the time for a pendulum's complete swing—that is, from one side, across to the other side, and back again—is proportional to the square root of the pendulum's length. The actual relationship is given by the equation

$$t = 2\pi \sqrt{\frac{l}{g}}$$

where t is the time and l is the length of the cord. Notice that the equation has two other symbols. One is π (pi), which often turns up when circles are involved, and the other symbol is g, the acceleration due to gravity.

Uses of pendulums

The first important application of the pendulum was to regulate the mechanism of a clock. Galileo suggested this, but the Dutch scientist Christiaan Huygens (1629-1695) built the first practical pendulum clocks in 1656. The swinging pendulum regulated an escapement, which was a wheel and ratchet arrangement that allowed other wheels to turn slowly, driven by a falling weight or by a spring.

TRY THIS

Swinging low

A weight swinging at the end of a thread or string is called a pendulum. This project looks at what happens if you change the size of the weight, and what happens if you change the length of the thread.

What to do

Cut a length of thread to the height of a table above the floor. Place two rulers together, trap the thread between them close to one end of the rulers, and tape the rulers together (at both ends). The idea is to be able to vary the length of the thread by pulling it between the two rulers. Place the rulers so that the thread end overhangs the edge of the table and hold them in place with a heavy book. You can now tie various weights to the lower end of the thread to make pendulums.

First, try a small washer. Tie it to the thread, pull it to one side, and then let go. Count the number of swings it makes in 10 seconds. It is easier if you have a helper to shout out when 10 seconds are up while you count the swings. Make a

note of the answer. Repeat the experiment with heavier weights, and again note how many swings occur in 10 seconds.

Choose another weight, say an eraser, and tie it to the thread. This time vary the length of the thread by pulling it through the rulers, again counting the number of swings in 10 seconds for each length of pendulum. Make a note of your findings.

You should find that the number of swings does not change when you vary the weight at the end of the thread. But the number does vary when you change the length of the thread. In fact, if you shorten the thread to one-fourth of its original length, the pendulum will swing twice as fast.

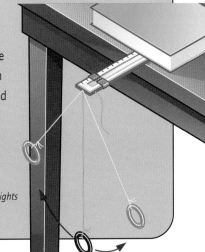

Time the swings with different weights and different lengths of string.

ENERGY, WORK, AND POWER

These three things—energy, work, and power—are sometimes confused. Energy is the ability to do work; work results when a force acts over a distance; and power is the rate of doing work. So we will begin with energy, of which there are various kinds.

When asked to do a chore at the end of a tiring day, we may say, "I can't—I don't have the energy." This is a fairly accurate statement, scientifically speaking. Energy is something that, possessed by something else, enables it to do work. As we will see, there are various kinds of energy. We cannot make it or destroy it, which is called the principle of conservation of energy. But we can use energy, and in doing so we change it from one of its forms to another form.

The water stored behind this dam represents a huge reserve of potential energy. As the water falls, the potential energy is converted to kinetic energy that can be made to do work by turning turbine blades.

The energy we use doing work comes from the food we eat. Food is essentially a mixture of chemicals. The processes of digestion change them into other chemicals, such as the high-energy sugar glucose. When we do work, our muscles use up glucose to provide energy.

Kinds of energy

Potential energy is energy that something has because of its position. A book on a shelf, for example, has energy stored in it as potential energy. It may look the same as a book on the floor; but if it is knocked off the shelf, the falling book can be made to do work. Imagine tying a string to the book and attaching the

KINDS OF ENERGY

Nine different kinds of energy are illustrated here, from the potential energy of the weights wound up in the clock to the awesome nuclear energy of an exploding atomic bomb, which releases vast quantities of heat, light, and sound.

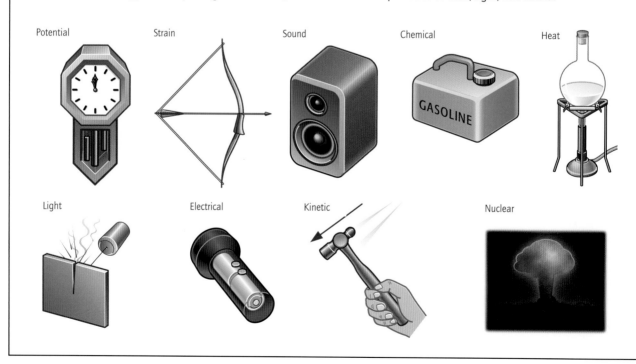

Potential
Strain
Sound
Chemical
Heat

Light
Electrical
Kinetic
Nuclear

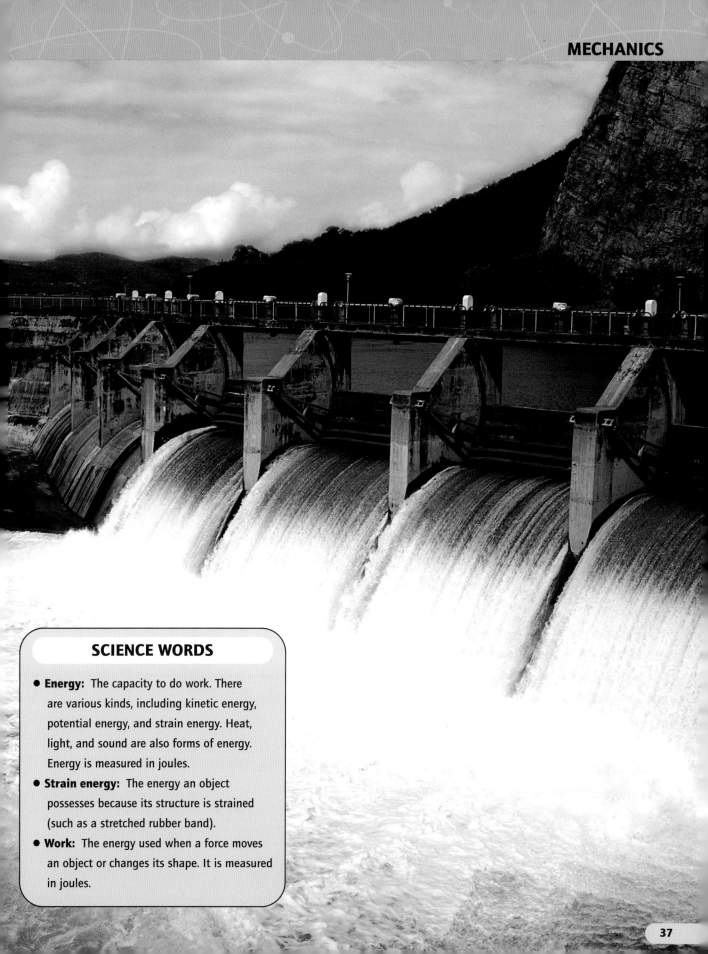

SCIENCE WORDS

- **Energy:** The capacity to do work. There are various kinds, including kinetic energy, potential energy, and strain energy. Heat, light, and sound are also forms of energy. Energy is measured in joules.
- **Strain energy:** The energy an object possesses because its structure is strained (such as a stretched rubber band).
- **Work:** The energy used when a force moves an object or changes its shape. It is measured in joules.

other end to a nearby vase. Knock the book off the shelf, and watch it do work on the vase! The water stored in a reservoir behind a dam has potential energy that can do work turning turbines to make electricity.

Strain energy is similar in some ways. When you wind up a clock or pull a bow, you strain the material of the spring or the bow and store energy in it. The clock spring slowly unwinds to work the clock, and the bow very rapidly straightens to speed an arrow to its target.

Kinetic energy is the energy of motion, so it is the form of energy possessed by anything that is moving. A swinging hammer has kinetic energy that can do the work of knocking a nail into a lump of wood. A speeding truck has lots of kinetic energy, which is why it can cause so much damage if it accidentally crashes into something.

Heat and light are also forms of energy. Anything that is hot possesses heat energy that can be made to do work in machines such as steam turbines and automobile engines. Green plants use light energy to combine carbon dioxide and water to form sugar and oxygen in the process known as photosynthesis, and light brings about other chemical reactions utilized in photography. The energy of the light in a laser beam is great enough to cut through metal.

Electrical energy is one of the most familiar types of energy. It is produced by batteries and by generators in

SCIENCE WORDS

- **Fission:** The splitting of a heavy atomic nucleus into two roughly equal parts, with the release of energy.
- **Fusion:** The merging of two light nuclei to form a heavier one, with the release of energy.

An archer stretches his bow and takes aim, about to convert the strain energy stored in the bow into the kinetic energy of a speeding arrow.

Like the ball in the basin on the right of this page, the people on the roller coaster switch between having mostly potential energy to mostly kinetic energy. They do retain some kinetic energy at the top of the ride because they keep moving.

power plants, and can be made to do all kinds of work from, for example, powering flashlights to driving railroad locomotives.

Sound is a form of energy that is seldom used directly for its energy, although ultrasound is used in medicine and industry to break up kidney stones and cut metals. Prolonged exposure to loud sounds can damage human hearing, sometimes permanently.

The chemical energy locked up in fuels is released when the fuels are burned to produce heat or light. Chemical energy is also released in batteries (but more slowly), where it is converted into electricity.

ROLLING BALLS

A ball rolling back and forth in a basin switches between having all potential energy (at the highest positions) and all kinetic energy (at the lowest position).

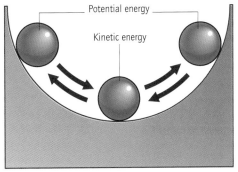

The final type of energy we need to know about is nuclear energy, produced by changes that take place in the nuclei of atoms. Energy is released in fission reactions when large nuclei (e.g. uranium) split into smaller ones. Nuclear energy also comes from fusion reactions in which light nuclei such as hydrogen nuclei combine to form heavier ones. Fusion reactions occur at the heart of the Sun and other stars, as well as in hydrogen bombs.

Interconversion of energy

We noted earlier that energy cannot be created or destroyed, merely changed from one form into another. A few examples should illustrate this point. The pendulum (pages 34 to 35) is an energy converter. When the pendulum bob is at one end of its swing it has potential energy (because of its position). As it swings across it gains kinetic energy (because it is moving). The potential energy is converted to kinetic energy, which is changed back to potential energy at the other end of the swing.

A speeding bullet also has kinetic energy. When it hits a hard target such as a wall, it stops, and the kinetic energy is converted into heat energy, as well as some sound energy. When a meteorite enters the Earth's atmosphere, friction with the air heats it up (heat energy), and it ionizes atoms in the atmosphere, creating a brief streak of light (light energy), which we see as a falling star.

The food we eat has chemical energy stored in it. This energy drives our body processes, keeps us warm, and is used up in our muscles whenever we do physical work.

James Joule

James Joule (1818-1889) was a British physicist best known for establishing the connections between electricity and heat and between mechanical energy and heat. In 1840, he announced what is now called Joule's law, which relates the electricity flowing in a wire and the wire's resistance to the amount of heat produced. Three years later, he worked out how much heat is produced by a given amount of mechanical work, by measuring the heat produced when a container of water was stirred by paddles driven by falling weights. For several years Joule worked with William Thomson (Lord Kelvin) (1824-1907), and between them they discovered the Joule-Thomson effect, in which a gas is cooled when it escapes through narrow holes.

Energy and work

The energy content of food is generally measured in joules (or calories). And the joule is the unit used for measuring every other form of energy—for example, heat and mechanical energy. It is possible to compare energy sources in terms of joules. The joule is also the unit for measuring work. In fact, 1 joule is equal to a force of 1 newton moving through a distance of 1 meter. Whenever a force moves something, work is done. For example, if I pick up off the floor a book weighing 20 newtons (i.e., it has a mass of about 2 kg) and place it on a shelf 0.5 m high, the work done by my muscles is 20 * 0.5 = 10 joules. But if I carry three books up a flight of stairs 4 meters high, the work I have done is 60 * 4 = 240 joules—much more tiring!

The sudden destructive release of chemical energy is evident in this detonation of blasting explosives in a quarry.

Work and power

Power is the rate of doing work. If I carried those three books upstairs in 12 seconds, the power would be 240 ÷ 12 = 20 joules per second. But if I ran up the stairs in just 4 seconds, the power would be 240 ÷ 4 = 60 joules per second. (Both of these sums neglect the power that is used in lifting me upstairs.) Although the above calculations give power in joules per second, in physics power has its own unit, the watt (1 watt = 1 joule per second), named after the Scottish engineer James Watt (1736-1819). So in my run upstairs, I converted energy at 60 watts—about the same as a dim electric light bulb.

SLOW AND FAST ELEVATORS

If these two elevators carry the same numbers of passengers, the express elevator needs four times as much power to move four times as fast as the slow elevator. It therefore needs a much larger electric motor to power its winding drum.

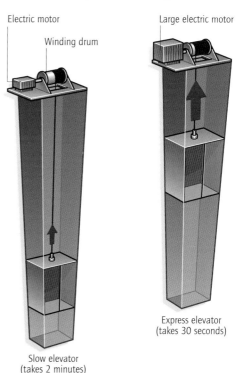

Electric motor

Winding drum

Large electric motor

Express elevator
(takes 30 seconds)

Slow elevator
(takes 2 minutes)

STABILITY AND EQUILIBRIUM

Normally, when a force acts on an object it makes it move in a straight line in the direction of the force. But in certain circumstances a force may have no effect at all, or cause the object to move in the arc of a circle, or even make it fall over.

The effect of a force on an object depends on how stable the object is. A cube-shaped box on a table top just sits there. It is perfectly stable and shows no tendency to move. If you tilt it slightly, raising one edge off the table, then let it go, it drops back down onto the table. In scientific terms, the box is said to be in stable equilibrium.

A cylinder lying on its side is slightly different. It will stay where it is put (if it is placed on a level surface, that is); but if given a slight push, it will roll along. Such an object is said to be in neutral equilibrium. But a narrow cylinder balanced on one end is different. Give it the slightest sideways tilt, and it topples over. It is in unstable equilibrium.

SCIENCE WORDS

- **Center of gravity:** Also called center of mass, the point at which an object's total mass appears to be concentrated and at which it acts.
- **Equilibrium:** A state of physical balance. If an object in stable equilibrium is tilted, its center of gravity rises, and when released, it falls back to its original position. If an object in neutral equilibrium is tilted, its center of gravity neither rises nor falls, and the object merely rolls. If an object in unstable equilibrium is tilted, its center of gravity falls, and the object will topple over.

Center of gravity

The point at which all of an object's mass appears to be concentrated is called its center of gravity (also sometimes called center of mass). In the cubical box, the center of gravity is right at the center. If you tilt the box, its center of gravity rises slightly. In the cylinder on its side, the center of gravity is halfway along its axis (the line joining the centers of each end). When the cylinder rolls, its center of gravity moves sideways, but does not move farther up or down.

The same cylinder standing on end has its center of gravity in the same place—halfway along its central axis. But this time, when the cylinder is tilted sideways, the center of gravity moves down slightly, and a

EQUILIBRIUM

The cube and the cone on its base are both in stable equilibrium, and each falls back onto its base if tilted. The ball and the cone on its side are both in neutral equilibrium and can roll. The cone on its point and the narrow cylinder are both in unstable equilibrium, and they topple if tilted far enough sideways.

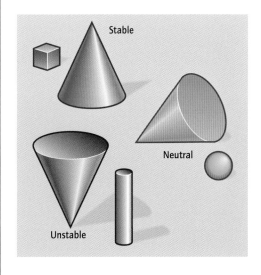

Stable

Neutral

Unstable

This precariously balanced rock—the result of centuries of erosion—is in unstable equilibrium. If it is tilted, it will topple over.

TRY THIS

Cheating the force of gravity

Whether or not an object can be balanced depends on where its center of gravity is. By setting up objects with unusual centers of gravity, you can seem to cheat the force of gravity.

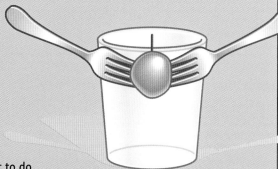

What to do

Make a small ball of modeling clay and carefully stick in two forks at an angle. Also *Carefully balance the forks on the rim of the drinking glass.* press a toothpick into the clay, as shown in the illustration. Now balance the whole arrangement on the edge of a drinking glass (you may have to move it slightly back and forth on the edge of the glass to find the best position). It looks like magic!

This "trick" is possible because the center of gravity is in the space between the handles of the forks. As long as the toothpick passes through this point, the whole arrangement will balance with the center of gravity on the edge of the glass.

Another way of demonstrating this is to stick the forks (handles downward) into a lump of modeling clay molded onto a pencil near the pointed end. This arrangement will balance on the point of the pencil—try it on the base of the upturned glass.

If you break off the pencil point and file a notch in the end with a nail file, you can balance it on a tightly stretched length of string, like a tightrope walker.

vertical line through it meets the table at a position outside the cylinder's base. This combination of circumstances makes the cylinder unstable, and it falls over.

So, the stability of an object depends on what happens to its center of gravity when it is tilted. If the center moves up, the object is in stable equilibrium. If the center moves sideways, it is in neutral equilibrium. But if the center moves down, the object is in unstable equilibrium.

Balancing forces

A seesaw represents a different kind of equilibrium. Think of a seesaw pivoted at its center. It balances on the pivot (which is called a fulcrum in physics) because there are equal weights on either side. But add unequal weights to each side—say a child at the end of one side and an adult at the end of the other—and the seesaw tips downward on the heavier side. The unequal forces (the weights of the people are forces) produce a turning effect. This effect is called a turning moment, and its size is equal to the force multiplied by its distance from the fulcrum.

So to balance the seesaw with the child and the adult, we have to make the turning moments the same. The only way to achieve this is for the adult to move

nearer the fulcrum so that the adult's weight multiplied by his distance to the fulcrum is the same as the product of the child's weight and her distance to the fulcrum.

By the way, because a turning moment is equal to a force (measured in newtons, N) multiplied by a distance (measured in meters, m), its units are newton-meters, written as Nm. A monkey wrench is a good example of a practical use of turning moments. When changing a wheel on a car with a flat tire, it is not possible to turn the wheel nuts using just your

SCIENCE WORDS

- **Couple:** The effect of two moments acting on an object in the same sense (i.e. both clockwise or both counter clockwise) at the same time.
- **Fulcrum:** A pivot, as on a seesaw or where a lever pivots.
- **Moment:** The turning effect (torque) produced when a force acts on an object, equal to the force multiplied by the perpendicular distance of its line of action to the pivot.

SIMPLE SEESAW

A seesaw is a simple example of turning moments. Children of equal weight balance at equal distances from the pivot. For an adult to have a ride, he or she has to sit closer to the pivot.

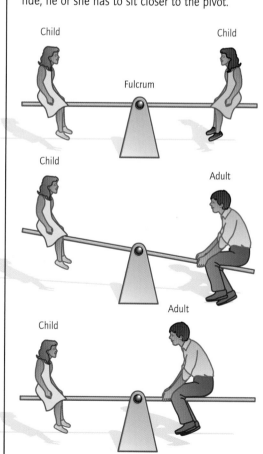

Child   Child
                Fulcrum

Child
                    Adult

                    Adult
Child

As long as this acrobat keeps his center of gravity (and that of the bowl on his head) over the cylinder below the board that is acting as a fulcrum, he will remain balanced.

tall narrow one because the distance from the handle to the hinges is greater.

Two are better than one

If there are two turning moments acting at the same point, the combined effect of both forces is called a couple. A familiar example is a faucet, which is turned by applying one moment on one side and an equal and opposite moment on the other side. Engineers sometimes use a long cylindrical wrench, called a socket wrench, for undoing stubborn nuts. It has a rod, termed a tommy bar, through one end of the cylinder. The other end goes over the nut, and the engineer applies a turning force to each end of the tommy bar. The turning effect of the couple unscrews the nut. A screwdriver is another example of a tool that uses couples. A screwdriver with a fat handle produces a greater couple and more turning force than one with a thin handle.

WRENCH AROUND

Applying a force F to the handle of a wrench at a distance d from the nut produces a turning moment Fd, also known as a torque.

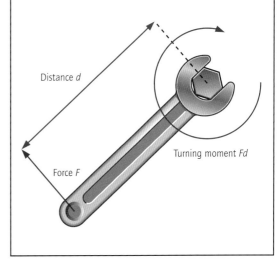

Distance d

Force F

Turning moment Fd

---

fingers—they are not strong enough. But using a wrench makes it easy because a force of 100 N applied at right angles to the handle of a wrench 25 cm long produces a turning moment of $100 * 0.25 = 25$ Nm. The crank between the pedal of a bicycle and the chain wheel acts in a similar way to produce rotation. You also use a turning moment whenever you open a door. It takes more force to open a short wide door than a

LOADS AND LEVERS

A lever is probably the simplest kind of machine, which we can define as any device that provides a mechanical advantage. But even though they are simple, there are three very different kinds of lever, which have dozens of applications.

The ancient Greek scientist Archimedes is reputed to have once said, "Give me a lever long enough and somewhere to stand, and I will move the Earth." Archimedes (*c.* 287–212 B.C.) certainly did make extensive use of levers in the various ingenious machines he designed for his patron, the king of Syracuse.

Three classes of lever

All kinds of lever have several things in common. They all involve a force, called the effort, that moves a load, making use of a pivot, or fulcrum. Archimedes' Earth-moving lever was a Class 1 lever, which works like a

crowbar. Scissors or shears make use of a pair of Class 1 levers. The effort and load act in the same direction on opposite sides of the fulcrum (see the illustration below).

In a Class 2 lever the effort and load are on the same side of the fulcrum and act in opposite directions. The load is nearer the fulcrum than the effort. A wheelbarrow is a familiar example of a Class 2 lever.

THREE CLASSES OF LEVER

The three classes of lever are Class 1, with load and effort on opposite sides of the fulcrum; Class 2, with load and effort on the same side, but the load nearer the fulcrum; and Class 3, with load and effort again on the same side, but the effort nearer the fulcrum.

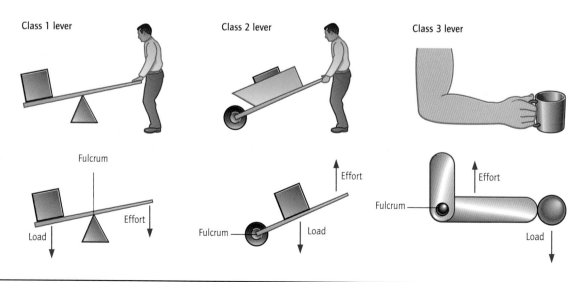

Class 1 lever

Class 2 lever

Class 3 lever

Fulcrum

Effort

Load

Effort

Fulcrum — Load

Effort

Fulcrum —

Load

Finally, a Class 3 lever also has the effort and the load on the same side and acting in opposite directions. But this time, the effort is nearer the fulcrum than the load is. The way your forearm works when you pick up something and the way tweezers and tongs work are examples of Class 3 levers in action. In fact, all movements of jointed bones in our bodies involve levers of one type or another.

Mechanical advantage

In a Class 1 lever, if the distance from the effort to the fulcrum is greater than the distance from the load to the fulcrum, then a small effort can move a large load. We say that the lever provides a mechanical advantage, which is defined as the load (output force) divided by the effort (input force). This ratio is also sometimes called the force ratio, and for a Class 1 lever it is equal to the distance from the effort to the fulcrum divided by the distance from the load to the fulcrum. It also equals the distance the effort moves divided by the distance the load moves.

For a lever or any other kind of machine to be useful, the mechanical advantage must be greater than 1. Imagine trying to pry the lid off a tin of paint using a coin as a kind of short crowbar. It acts as a Class 1

A pole-vaulter's pole acts as a lever to lift him into the air. The vaulter also gets help from the springiness of the pole.

A pair of garden shears, like scissors, consists of a pair of Class 1 levers working together. The longer the handles, the greater the mechanical advantage.

lever with a mechanical advantage of about 4. (Because mechanical advantage is a ratio of two forces, it is a pure number and has no units.) If this is not enough to remove the lid, you can greatly increase the mechanical advantage by using a screwdriver to pry off the lid—like a long crowbar. This will provide a mechanical advantage of up to 30, which should be more than enough to open it. The illustrations on these pages show other examples of various levers in action.

Wheel and axle

A windlass is a device that uses a handle to turn a cylindrical drum to wind a bucket up from a well.

A dump truck tipping its load is an everyday instance of a Class 2 lever in action.

DUMP TRUCK

The hydraulic mechanism of this dump truck is an example of a Class 2 lever. Compare it with the wheelbarrow on page 46.

Pivot

Effort

Load

A capstan used to pull up the anchor chain on a ship is another example. In scientific terms, such a device is called a wheel and axle. It is a variety of Class 1 lever in which the effort can be applied continuously.

The input force is applied at the rim of the wheel, and the output force acts at the rim of the axle. If the wheel has a radius of R units and the axle has a radius of r units, the mechanical advantage is R divided by r. A car's steering wheel is another everyday example of a wheel and axle.

Mechanical efficiency

All these devices that use levers are examples of simple machines. Some perform better than others—that is, some machines are more efficient than others. Efficiency is the energy (or power) produced by a machine, the useful work done, divided by the energy (or power) it consumes. It is usually expressed as a

WHEEL AND AXLE

A wheel and axle are used in a windlass for raising a bucket from a well. This can provide a large mechanical advantage.

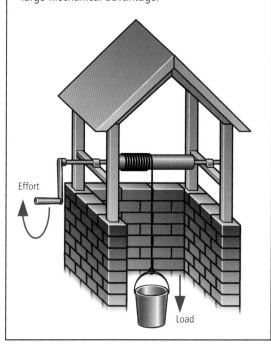

Effort

Load

LEVERING UPWARD

The cork lifter, or bottle opener, also employs a pair of Class 1 levers. The load is very close to the fulcrum, producing a large mechanical advantage that should shift the most stubborn cork.

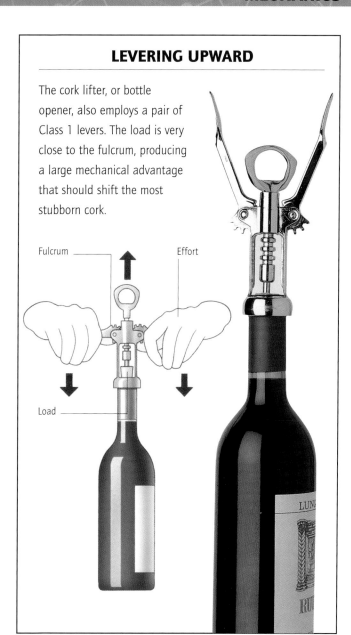

Fulcrum

Effort

Load

percentage and is always less than 100 percent since no machine is perfect.

In practice, there is usually a difference between any machine's theoretical mechanical advantage and its actual mechanical advantage. The ratio of these two—actual divided by theorectical—is also a measure of efficiency. A simple Class 1 lever is one of the most efficient machines, with an efficiency approaching 100 percent. Other simple machines, such as a screw (see page 52), are extremely inefficient.

INCLINES AND FRICTION

It is much easier to push a load up a slope than to lift it directly upward. The slope is called an inclined plane, and it is another example of a simple machine that provides a mechanical advantage. Without it the Ancient Egyptians could not have built the pyramids, and screws and bolts would not work.

Given the choice between a steep path straight up a hill or a gentle slope winding upward around it, most people would choose the gentler slope. Similarly, it is easier to climb a set of stairs than a vertical ladder. We do not think of such simple devices as machines, but they are to a physicist. They are examples of an inclined plane.

We have seen that a successful machine provides a mechanical advantage greater than 1. For an inclined plane the mechanical advantage is the load (a downward force) divided by the effort (the force pushing the load up the slope), which is equal to the length of the plane divided by the height of the slope.

The spiral staircase that winds up the outside of this observation tower makes it much easier to climb than a straight ladder.

SCIENCE WORDS

- **Friction:** A force that prevents or slows the movement of one surface against another surface.
- **Inclined plane:** A simple machine consisting of a ramp; the effort is used to push a load up the ramp. A wedge used to split things is also an inclined plane.
- **Mechanical advantage:** Also called force ratio, in a simple machine it is the load divided by the effort.

A wedge is a simple application of the inclined plane. Imagine driving a wedge under the edge of a heavy block. As the wedge moves in, it gradually lifts the block. This is exactly similar to pushing a block up an inclined plane, and the mechanical advantage is equal to the length of the wedge divided by its maximum thickness. Wedges have many uses, from splitting logs and rocks to forming the cutting part of an ax or chisel. All other cutting tools, from saws to sandpaper, make use of the action of wedges.

The Ancient Egyptians are thought to have built huge earth ramps—inclined planes—spiraling around the pyramids while they were building them. Slaves hauled large blocks of stone weighing many tons up the ramps, probably on rollers to reduce friction between the blocks and the ramp. When the pyramid was finished, after many years of back-breaking work, the ramps were finally dismantled and the earth taken away to reveal the completed structure.

Spiral inclined planes

Winding a wedge (an inclined plane) around a cylinder can create much smaller spiral ramps. The result is a screw thread. When a screw is rotated in a block of

There is very little friction between a skater's skates and the ice. That is because the pressure on the skates (because of the skater's weight) melts the ice slightly and provides a film of lubricating water.

wood, its threads cut into the wood and draw in the screw. Screws are tapered, but parallel-sided bolts work in the same way. The long narrow wedge that forms the thread makes a large mechanical advantage. Its value depends on the pitch of the screw, which is the distance it travels forward in one compete rotation. This, in turn, is equal to the distance between the screw's threads.

Overcoming friction

A screw remains in a piece of wood because of friction. Friction is a force that tends to prevent stationary

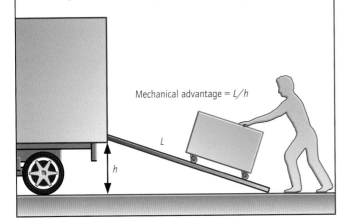

INCLINED PLANE

It is easier to push a load up an inclined plane than to lift it up vertically. The mechanical advantage equals the length of the ramp (L) divided by its height (h).

Mechanical advantage = L/h

SCREWS AND JACKS

The mechanical advantage of a screw depends on its pitch, the distance between its threads. Rotating a screw enables it to lift things. This is the principle of the jackscrew, as used for lifting an automobile to change a tire.

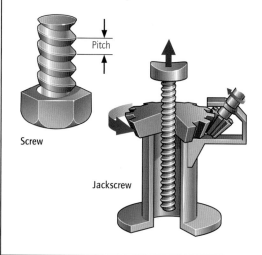

Screw

Jackscrew

STATIC FRICTION

Static friction—the force needed to start an object sliding along a surface—depends on the object's weight, not on its shape or the area of contact between the object and the surface. All the objects shown here have the same weight (*W*), and static friction is the same for all of them. Lubricants reduce friction by introducing a layer of softer substance between the object and the surface.

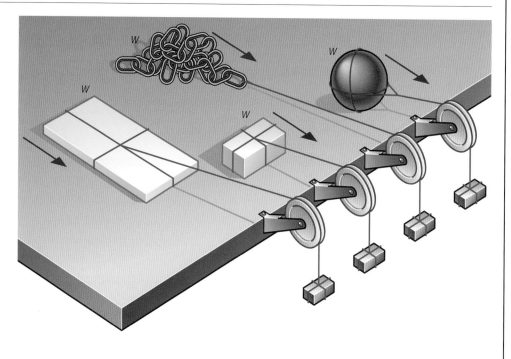

A technician using an angle grinder with a friction blade to cut through sheet steel. This type of saw uses its high speed of rotation to generate heat through friction in order to soften the metal in front of the blade, making it much easier to cut.

objects in contact from moving. Without it a screw would unscrew itself. But in the moving parts of machines friction is a nuisance, representing a waste of energy—for example, it soaks up about half the power of an automobile engine. Oil, grease, and other lubricants between the moving parts are designed to reduce friction.

A strange low-temperature effect is called superfluidity. This term describes a fluid, such as liquid helium a few degrees above absolute zero (0 K, −273°C or −460°F), that flows without friction. Placed in a container, liquid helium flows vertically up the sides, over the lip, and escapes. On a slope, it flows uphill against the force of gravity. So far scientists have found no practical uses for such superfluids.

TRY THIS

Keep on rolling

Some ancient peoples moved huge heavy objects without any modern equipment. More than 3,000 years ago, the Ancient Egyptians built the pyramids from large blocks of stone. They probably dragged the blocks, using hundreds of slaves. To make the blocks move more easily, they probably used rollers. This project uses the Egyptians' methods.

What to do

Put a book on a table. Make a loose loop of string, and put it around the book, as shown in the illustration, and tie a rubber band to the string. Now pull the book along by the rubber band. The amount the rubber band stretches is a measure of how much force you have to use. Now arrange six round pencils or marker pens as a set of rollers, and put the book on top of them. Pull the book again, and notice how you do not have to use so much force.

The force you have to overcome to get the book moving is friction. Sliding friction, as between the book and the table, is greater than the rolling friction between the pencils (or pens) and the table. Try placing a second book on top of the first one. Are the two books harder to move?

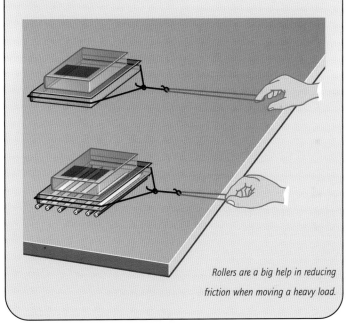

Rollers are a big help in reducing friction when moving a heavy load.

PULLEYS AND GEARS

Lifting heavy loads was a problem for ancient peoples, whose only help was the inclined plane and, later, the jackscrew. The problem was solved with the invention of pulleys. Later, gears were used to control the output of rotating machinery.

Most people today think of a machine as a useful device with wheels, gears, and other rotating parts. In many ways this idea is correct, although some modern machines (such as an electrical transformer) have no moving parts. We have seen levers and other simple machines on the previous pages, and nearly all of them were devised to help lift a load. One of the best lifting machines is a pulley.

Pulleys and pulling

The simplest pulley has a rope passing over a single grooved wheel, like the type a farmer might use to haul a bale of hay up to the hayloft. In fact, a single pulley is not really a machine at all. Its mechanical advantage (the distance moved by the effort divided by the distance moved by the load) is 1, so there is no real advantage at all. And it cannot be used for lifting anything heavier than the person pulling on the rope. All the single pulley does is to change the direction of a force—the downward pull on the rope lifts up the load.

But with two or more pulleys together, the situation is different. Two pulleys give a mechanical advantage of 2, three pulleys give a mechanical advantage of 3, and so on. The number of pulley wheels, or more precisely the number of ropes between them, produces the mechanical advantage of multiple pulleys, usually known as a block and tackle. With three wheels, however, the effort has to move three times as far as the load is lifted. As a result, a lot of rope has to be pulled through the pulley block to raise the load a small distance. Such pulleys came into their own in

On this heavy-duty winding mechanism the smaller gear in front turns faster than the larger gear it drives.

the days of sailing ships, when they were used to haul up the heavy weight of large canvas sails. They still have many uses today, especially in the large cranes that are used for lifting heavy loads on construction sites and at shipyards.

Belts and gears

Early sources of power included water wheels and windmills. They needed a way of transferring the rotation of a shaft to other machines, such as millstones for grinding grain. One method was to link a wheel on the driven shaft to a wheel on the other machine using a rope or belt. Ropes ran on grooved wheels (like pulleys), and belts ran over wheels with flat rims. Belt drives were still in use long after the invention of the steam engine for connecting this new source of power to mechanized looms and metalworking machinery. The fan belt on an automobile, which enables the engine to turn the shaft of the electric generator, is a modern example of a belt drive.

By varying the sizes of the wheels—the drive wheel and the driven wheel—the speed of rotation could be changed. A large drive wheel turns a smaller driven wheel faster, whereas a small drive wheel turns a

---

SCIENCE WORDS

- **Block and tackle:** A multiple pulley, one with two or more pulley wheels.
- **Machine:** A device that allows one force (the effort) to overcome another (the load).
- **Pulley:** A simple machine consisting of a fixed grooved wheel with a rope running around it. A mechanical advantage of more than 1 can be achieved only by using two or more pulleys together.

larger driven wheel slower. Both wheels rotate in the same direction, unless the belt has a half turn like a figure eight.

Larger and smaller wheels were also used when gears began to replace belt drives. Gears, also called cogwheels or cogs, are toothed wheels, usually on parallel shafts, positioned so that the teeth of one engage with the teeth of the other. Again, a large drive gear turns a smaller gear (called a pinion) faster, and a small drive gear turns a larger gear slower. The two gears rotate in opposite directions. To make the pinion gear rotate in the same direction as the drive gear, a free-running idler gear is introduced between the two.

SINGLE AND MULTIPLE PULLEYS

A single pulley only changes the direction of the pull on the rope. A multiple pulley, or block and tackle, provides a mechanical advantage. With four pulleys and four ropes between them the mechanical advantage is 4. The same pull P as with the single pulley will lift a load that is four times as heavy.

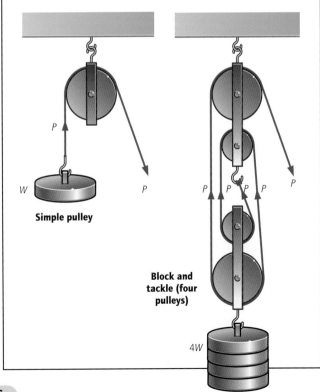

Simple pulley

Block and tackle (four pulleys)

Mobile cranes dominate the skyline at a dockyard, where they are used to lift heavy cargoes into or out of ships' holds. All the lifting movements are achieved using pulleys.

Other kinds of gear

A pinion gear driving a straight rod with teeth cut in it, called a rack, produces a side-to-side movement. It is called a rack and pinion, and is used in the steering mechanism of an automobile. A gear cut like a screw thread, called a helical gear or worm gear, can turn another gear on a shaft at right angles to it. Another way of changing the direction of rotation through a right angle is to use bevel gears, which are cut on an angle. Bevel gears are used, for example, in differential drives of automobiles to transmit power to two axles spinning at different speeds, such as in cornering. (See (d), (e), and (f) in the illustration on the opposite page for these three different types.)

CROWN WHEEL AND PINION

When a truck or car goes around a curve, the wheel on the outer side of the curve goes farther, and rotates more, than the wheel on the inside of the curve. This arrangement allows it to happen.

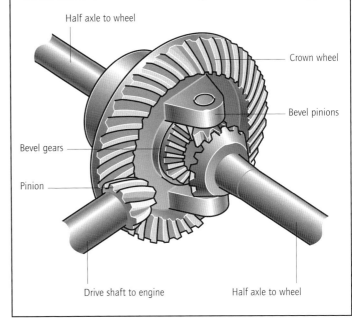

Half axle to wheel
Crown wheel
Bevel pinions
Bevel gears
Pinion
Drive shaft to engine
Half axle to wheel

DIFFERENT KINDS OF GEAR

Shown here are (a) a drive gear turning a faster pinion in the opposite direction, (b) the use of an idler gear to keep the direction of rotation the same, (c) a small drive gear turning the driven gear slower, (d) a rack and pinion, (e) a helical gear, and (f) bevel gears.

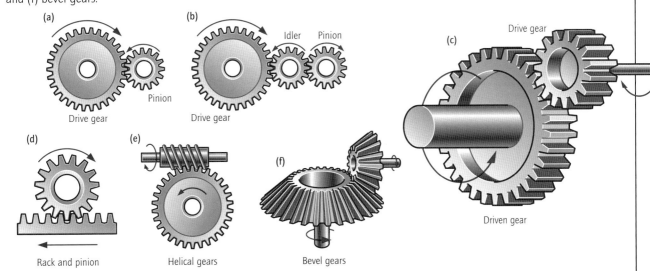

(a) Drive gear / Pinion
(b) Idler / Pinion / Drive gear
(c) Drive gear / Driven gear
(d) Rack and pinion
(e) Helical gears
(f) Bevel gears

STRAINS ON SOLIDS

Solids can resist deforming forces much better than gases and liquids can. But there is a limit even to the strength of solids—if you strain them enough, they will break. For lower strains they will return to their normal shape when the strain is removed.

Two key properties of most solids are strength and hardness. Nowhere are these properties used to better effect than in the construction industry. Over the ages, the chief permanent materials for construction have been stone, brick, concrete, and steel. They can be compared by considering how builders and engineers have solved the problem of building over a space to make a bridge.

The earliest material for bridges, not counting tree trunks and vines, was stone. The simplest stone bridge consists of a single slab across two supports, called a post-and-beam construction. But the length of such a span is limited to the longest piece of stone available. Masonry—square-cut pieces of stone—and its artificial imitator, brick, were next to be used. And the secret of using these materials for spans is the arch. Many of the arches built in ancient Egypt, Greece, and Rome are still standing today.

This three-tiered arch bridge, the Pont du Gard at Nîmes, is a Roman aqueduct. It was built of stone across a valley in southern France.

SCIENCE WORDS

- **Ductile:** Describing a metal that can easily be drawn out to form wire.
- **Elasticity:** The property of a solid that enables it to return to its original shape after it is stretched (that is, after it has been subjected to stress).
- **Strain:** The change in shape of a solid object when it is subjected to a stress.
- **Stress:** A force that tends to change the shape of a solid object, producing strain.

An arch is a sturdy structure because the materials making it are strong in compression—that is, when they are being squeezed. Each stone in an arch is in compression, and together they carry the load to the arch supports. Concrete also has good compressive strength. But reinforced concrete, which has steel rods within its structure, is also strong in tension (when it is

BRIDGE CONSTRUCTION

The three main kinds of bridges differ in the way compressive forces are set up. The decks of the post-and-beam (a) and cantilever (b) are also under tension.

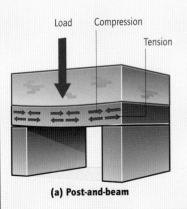

Load Compression

Tension

(a) Post-and-beam

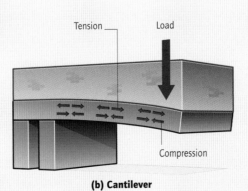

Tension Load

Compression

(b) Cantilever

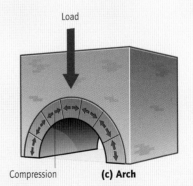

Load

Compression **(c) Arch**

being stretched). A cantilever bridge is built into supports at each end. When it is loaded, a cantilever beam is in tension on the top and under compression beneath. Reinforced concrete is a good material for making bridges in this way.

Steel is also strong in both tension and compression, and can be used for all types of construction. There is a practical limit to the length of a steel girder, but this limitation is overcome by making trusses. Several short girders are joined together to make a rigid structure formed of triangles. Trusses are also much lighter in weight than any solid construction.

Elastic metal

One property of steel and most other metals is elasticity. In scientific terms, an elastic material is one that stretches under tension, but returns to its original length when the tension is released. This property is very obvious with rubber and some plastics, which are collectively known as elastomers. But metals are also elastic, up to a point. That point is called the yield point. Imagine adding weights to the end of a

Robert Hooke

The English astronomer, physicist and engineer Robert Hooke (1635-1703) was the son of a clergyman. One of his earliest and most momentous insights in astronomy was his theory that the planets are held in their orbits by gravity, which he formulated in 1664. This became the subject of a dispute with Isaac Newton (1642-1727), who laid claim to the idea. Hooke's major contributions to physics were the law that bears his name and his discovery that most materials expand on heating. A master technician, Hooke also constructed a compound microscope for studying microscopic animals and plant shells, publishing his findings in the work *Micrographia* (1665). Other inventions included the "universal joint", a device that couples a rotating shaft to another shaft aligned at an angle.

HOOKE'S LAW

As a metal sample is stretched, the load (stress) is proportional to the elongation (strain) up to the elastic limit. This is Hooke's law. Beyond the yield point the sample stretches rapidly until it snaps at the breaking point.

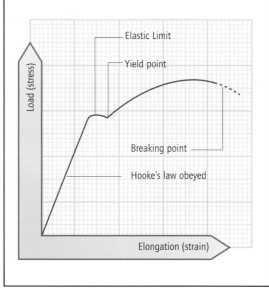

length of wire fixed to a support at its upper end. As more weights are added, the wire stretches. If the weights are removed, the wire returns to its original length. In fact, the stress on the wire (the weight) is proportional to the strain (the amount it stretches). This relationship is known as Hooke's law, after the English scientist Robert Hooke (1635-1703), who formulated it in 1676.

If we keep on adding weights to the end of the wire, a point will be reached—called the elastic limit— where the wire does not return to its original length. It is permanently stretched. Beyond the elastic limit, at the yield point, the wire continues to stretch with very little extra load until it finally breaks.

Wire for strength

A metal that is ductile can be pulled out to form wire. That is usually done in stages by pulling the wire through a series of dies. Each die is slightly smaller than the previous one, which makes the wire gradually become thinner.

Wire has many practical uses, particularly as a conductor of electricity. But wire is also used in construction. Several strands of wire can be twisted together to make a cable. Such cables are stronger than a single strand of the same thickness. Their most spectacular use is in suspension bridges, in which two or more long cables hang in an arc between two towers. Other thinner cables hang down from them to support a deck, which may be a roadway or a railroad.

Alloys for hardness

As well as their density, most metals are also known for their hardness. This property results from the tight packing of the atoms in the crystals that form metals. Soft metals, such as aluminum and iron, can be made hard by alloying them with other elements, which modifies their crystal structure. Aluminum is mixed with magnesium or copper, and iron is alloyed with carbon to produce steel.

KINDS OF STRESS

The three main kinds of stress are compression, when a material is squeezed; tension, when it is stretched; and shear, when the top and bottom are pulled in opposite directions.

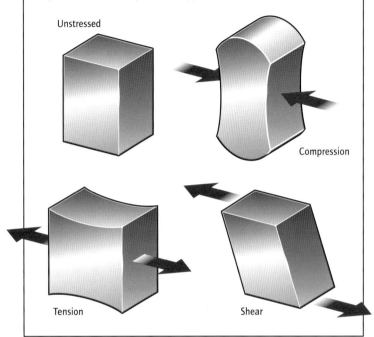

Unstressed

Compression

Tension

Shear

WINDING WIRE

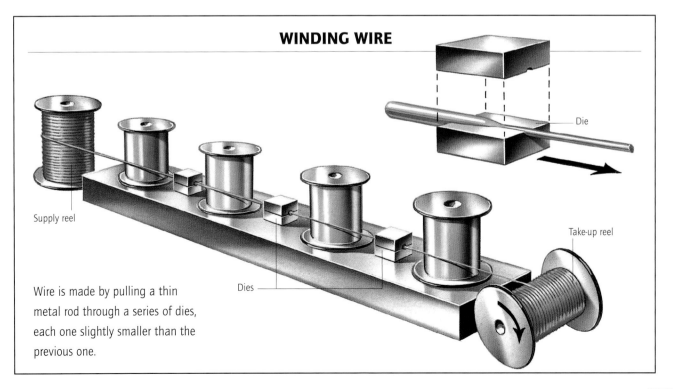

Supply reel

Die

Take-up reel

Dies

Wire is made by pulling a thin metal rod through a series of dies, each one slightly smaller than the previous one.

GLOSSARY

Acceleration The rate of change in a moving object's velocity. It is a vector quantity.

Air resistance A force, also called drag or wind resistance, which resists the movement of an object passing through the air. It is overcome by streamlining.

Atomic number The number of protons in an element's nucleus. The atomic number equals the number of electrons in the normal atom and is the element's numerical position in the periodic table.

Calutron A large mass spectrometer used for separating the isotopes of uranium.

Center of gravity Also called center of mass, the point at which an object's total mass appears to be concentrated and at which it acts.

Centrifugal force A fictitious force sometimes said to act in opposition to (and therefore to balance) the centripetal force.

Centrifuge A machine with a fast-spinning chamber that creates strong "artificial gravity" to separate materials of different densities.

Centripetal force The force that acts inward to keep an object moving in a circle.

Couple The effect of two moments acting on an object in the same sense (i.e. both clockwise or both counter clockwise) at the same time.

Ductile Describing a metal that can easily be drawn out to form wire.

Elasticity The property of a solid that enables it to return to its original shape after it has been stretched (that is, after it has been subjected to stress).

Electron A negatively charged elementary particle found in every atom.

Energy The capacity to do work. There are various kinds, including kinetic energy, potential energy, and strain energy. Heat, light, and sound are also forms of energy. Energy is measured in joules, a derived SI unit.

Equilibrium A state of physical balance.

Fission The splitting of a heavy atomic nucleus into two roughly equal parts, with the release of much energy.

Force An influence that changes the shape, position, or movement of an object.

Friction A force that prevents or slows the movement of one surface against another.

Fulcrum A pivot, as on a seesaw or where a lever pivots.

Fusion The merging of two light nuclei to form a heavier one, with the release of energy.

Gas diffusion A technology used in the enrichment of materials used in nuclear reactors and nuclear weapons.

Inclined plane A simple machine consisting of a ramp; the effort is used to push a load up the ramp. A wedge used to split things is also an inclined plane.

Inertia The property of an object that makes it tend to resist being moved or, if moving, to resist a change in direction. It is a consequence of the first of Newton's laws of motion.

Ion An atom or molecule that has lost or gained one or more electrons, so gaining an electric charge.

Isotope Any of the varieties of a chemical element that are chemically identical to one another, but whose atoms differ in their relative atomic mass.

joule (J) The derived SI unit of energy equal to the amount of work done when a force of 1 newton acts through a distance of 1 meter.

Kinetic energy The energy an object possesses because it is moving.

Load In a simple machine, the output force (such as that applied by the effort).

Luminous intensity The light-emitting power of a source of light.

Machine A device that allows one force (the effort) to overcome another (the load).

Mass The amount of matter in an object.

Mass spectrograph An instrument that separates fast-moving ions in a beam according to their mass.

Mechanical advantage Also called force ratio, in a simple machine it is the load divided by the effort.

Moment The turning effect (torque) produced when a force acts on an object, equal to the force multiplied by the perpendicular distance of its line of action to the pivot.

Momentum The mass of an object multiplied by its velocity in a straight line.

newton (N) The derived SI unit of force. It is the force required to give a mass of 1 kilogram an acceleration of 1 meter per second per second.

Potential energy The energy an object possesses because of its position (such as a weight that has been raised to a certain height above the ground).

Pulley A simple machine consisting of a fixed grooved wheel with a rope running around it.

Relative atomic mass The mass of an atom expressed in atomic mass units (amu). The atomic mass unit is defined as one-twelfth of the mass of the common isotope of carbon and is approximately equal to the mass of the hydrogen atom.

Scalar A quantity that has magnitude, but (unlike a vector) no specified direction. Examples of scalars are speed and mass.

SI units System of units used internationally in science (short for Système International d'Unités, its name in French). There are seven base units (ampere, candela, kelvin, kilogram, meter, mole, and second) and various derived units, which are combinations of base units.

Strain The change in shape of a solid object when it is subjected to a stress.

Strain energy The energy an object possesses because its structure is strained (such as a stretched rubber band).

Stress A force that tends to change the shape of a solid object, producing strain.

Terminal speed The maximum speed at which an object falls under the influence of gravity.

Thermocouple Temperature-measuring device comprising two wires of different metals joined at their ends.

Vector A quantity that has magnitude and (unlike a scalar) direction. Examples of vectors are acceleration and velocity.

Weight The force with which a mass is drawn toward the Earth (by the force of gravity).

Work The energy used when a force moves an object or changes its shape, measured in joules.

FURTHER RESEARCH

Books – General

Bloomfield, Louis A. *How Things Work: The Physics of Everyday Life.* Hoboken, NJ: Wiley, 2009.

Bloomfield, Louis A. *How Everything Works: Making Physics Out of the Ordinary.* Hoboken, NJ: Wiley, 2007.

Daintith, John. *A Dictionary of Physics.* New York, NY: Oxford University Press, 2010.

De Pree, Christopher. *Physics Made Simple.* New York, NY: Broadway Books, 2005.

Epstein, Lewis Carroll. *Thinking Physics: Understandable Practical Reality.* San Francisco, CA: Insight Press, 2009.

Glencoe McGraw-Hill. *Introduction to Physical Science.* Blacklick, OH: Glencoe/McGraw-Hill, 2007.

Heilbron, John L. *The Oxford Guide to the History of Physics and Astronomy.* New York, NY: Oxford University Press, 2005.

Holzner, Steve. *Physics Essentials For Dummies.* Hoboken, NJ: For Dummies, 2010.

Jargodzk, Christopher, and Potter, Franklin. *Mad About Physics: Braintwisters, Paradoxes, and Curiosities.* Hoboken, NJ: Wiley, 2000.

Lehrman, Robert L. *E-Z Physics.* Hauppauge, NY: Barron's Educational, 2009.

Lloyd, Sarah. *Physics: IGCSE Revision Guide.* New York, NY: Oxford University Press, 2009.

Suplee, Curt. *Physics in the 20th Century.* New York, NY: Harry N. Abrams, 2002.

Taylor, Charles (ed). *The Kingfisher Science Encyclopedia,* Boston, MA: Kingfisher Books, 2006.

Walker, Jearl. *The Flying Circus of Physics.* Hoboken, NJ: Wiley, 2006.

Watts, Lisa et al. *The Most Explosive Science Book in the Universe... by the Brainwaves.* New York, NY: DK Publishing, 2009.

Zitzewitz, Paul W. *Physics Principles and Problems.* Columbus, OH: McGraw-Hill, 2005.

Books – Mechanics

Arnold, Nick, and De Saulles, Tony. *Fatal Forces (Horrible Science).* New York, NY: Scholastic, 2008.

Cobb, Vicki. *Why Doesn't the Earth Fall Up? and Other Not Such Dumb Questions about Motion.* New York, NY: Scholastic, 2001.

DiSpezio, Michael Anthony. *Awesome Experiments in Force and Motion.* New York, NY: Sterling, 2006.

Kleppner, Daniel, and Kolenkow, Robert J. *An Introduction to Mechanics.* New York, NY: Cambridge University Press, 2010.

Lafferty, Peter. *Force & Motion (Eyewitness Books).* New York, NY: DK Publishing, 2000.

Padilla, Michael J. et al. *Prentice Hall Science Explorer: Motion, Forces, And Energy.* Upper Saddle River, NJ: Pearson Prentice Hall, 2006.

Web Sites

Marvellous machines
www.galaxy.net/~k12/machines/index.shtml
Experiments about simple machines.

How Stuff Works – Physical Science
http://science.howstuffworks.com/physical-science-channel.htm
Topics on all aspects of physics.

PhysLink.com
www.physlink.com/SiteInfo/Index.cfm
Physics and astronomy education, research, and reference.

PhysicsCentral
www.physicscentral.com/about/index.cfm
Education site of the American Physical Society.

Physics 2000
www.colorado.edu/physics/2000/index.pl
An interactive journey through modern physics.

The Why Files
http://whyfiles.org/
The science behind the news.

INDEX

Words and page numbers in **bold type** indicate main references to the various topics. Page numbers in *italic* refer to illustrations; those underlined refer to definitions. Page numbers in brackets indicate box features.

JAN 17 2012